W9-CVW-549

Beyond the Rainbow Bridge

A Thoughtful Guide for Coping with the Loss of a Horse

BY KIMBERLY GATTO

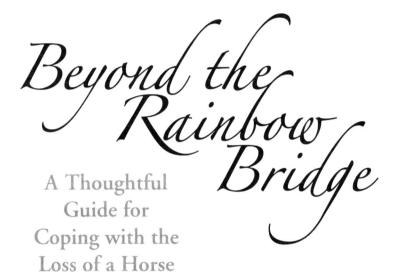

Beyond the Rainbow Bridge

A Thoughtful Guide for Coping with the Loss of a Horse

BY KIMBERLY GATTO

Foreword by Lynn Palm

Lisa Keer Carusone,
Contributing Editor

HALF HALT PRESS
BOONSBORO, MARYLAND

Beyond the Rainbow Bridge:
A Thoughtful Guide for
Coping with the Loss of a Horse

Published in the United States of America by

 Half Halt Press, Inc.
P.O. Box 67
Boonsboro, MD 21713
www.halfhaltpress.com

Cover, interior design and photo treatment by Design Point, Salisbury, NH
Photographs by Helen Peppe
Editorial services by Stacey Wigmore

"Zip Always Belonged to God" by John Lyons
reprinted with the kind permission of *The Perfect Horse*.

Story of Calypso and Melanie Smith Taylor
reprinted by the kind permission of Nancy Jaffer.

Printed in the United States of America

Library of Congress Cataloging-in-Publication Data

Gatto, Kimberly.
    Beyond the rainbow bridge : a thoughtful guide for coping with the loss of a horse / by
Kimberly Gatto ; foreword by Lynn Palm ; Lisa Keer Carusone, contributing editor.
        p. cm.
    ISBN 0-939481-71-5 (hardback)
        1. Horse owners--Psychology. 2. Pets--Death--Psychological aspects. 3.
Bereavement--Psychological aspects. I. Carusone, Lisa Keer. II. Title.

SF284.4G38 2005
155.9'37--dc22

2005052672

The Rainbow Bridge for Horses

By the edge of a woods, at the foot of a hill,
is a lush, green meadow where time stands still.
Where the friends of man and woman do run,
when their time on earth is over and done.

For here, between this world and the next,
is a place where beloved equines find rest.
On this golden land, they wait and they play,
'til The Rainbow Bridge they cross over one day.

No more do they suffer, in pain or in sadness,
for here they are whole, their lives filled with gladness.
Their limbs are restored, their health renewed.
Their bodies have healed with strength imbued.

They trot through the grass without even a care,
'til one day they whinny and sniff at the air.
All ears prick forward, eyes sharp and alert.
Then all of a sudden, one breaks from the herd.

For just at that second, there's no room for remorse.
As they see each other ... one person ... one horse.
So they run to each other, these friends from long past,
The time of their parting is over at last.

The sadness they felt while they were apart
has turned to joy once more in each heart.
They nuzzle with a love that will last forever.
And then, side-by-side, they cross over ... together.

— Author Unknown

FOREWORD   11

INTRODUCTION   15

Timely Writer   *17*

PROLOGUE   21

PART I: THE LOSS OF A HORSE

SoBo's Story   *27*

The Grieving Process   33

A Consolation   *41*

Coping with Sudden Loss   45

PART II: CROSSING THE BRIDGE

Skippy's Gifts   *55*

Euthanasia: A Veterinarian's Perspective   59

Preparing for Goodbye   65

Letting Go   71

PART III: THE FINAL FAREWELL

Falstaff   *81*

Burial, Cremation and Other Options   85

PART IV: CHILDREN AND LOSS

Forget-Me-Not   97

The Grieving Process for Children   103

PART V: WHEN HORSES GRIEVE

Rhino   111

Horses and Loss   115

PART VI: REMEMBERING A SPECIAL HORSE

Zip Always Belonged to God   123

Honoring a Horse's Memory   125

PART VII: OTHER TYPES OF LOSS

Loss Other Than Death   135

PART VIII: BEYOND THE RAINBOW BRIDGE

Loving Another Horse   151

A New Beginning   155

Resources   163

Notes   165

About the Author   167

Contributing Editor   169

Contributors   171

FOREWORD

By Lynn S. Palm

After I lost Rugged Lark in late 2004, I was asked what his passing meant to me. In my work as a trainer, teacher, rider and competitor, I'm usually ready for almost any question, but I had to think for a moment about that one.

What it meant to me was the realization that throughout my years with Rugged Lark, we'd had some real fun together. Sure, a big part of that fun was winning AQHA Super Horse titles and World Championships. Our demonstration ride at the 1996 Atlanta Olympics let us show the world what kind training methods, a happy horse and a great horse and rider partnership can look like.

But as I looked back, fun also meant things that were a little less glamorous, like those Christmas photos we took of him driving my antique sleigh. Or some great trail rides we enjoyed with friends. And, how could I forget, the trips to the pond for some swimming. He was, and is, "One Moment in Time." He brought out the best in me, and I'll never forget him.

Professional or amateur, we all have something in common when it comes to losing a horse. The experience touches each of us in similar ways. As you read this book, remember that even if you feel like you are alone with your loss, new or not so new, you have company. I've been there. I know how you feel, I know how you hurt and I know that, in time, you will do what I did and move on to start a new journey with another horse.

Having a horse in your life is a great gift. Those who truly have a passion for the horse will always feel the loss. It is the risk we take when we let horses into our lives.

Looking back at Rugged Lark and the other horses that have touched my life, I can say that it really has been a risk worth taking. ❧

INTRODUCTION

Somewhere ...
Somewhere in time's own space
There must be some sweet pastured place
Where creeks sing on and tall trees grow,
Some paradise where horses go.
For by the love that guides my pen
I know great horses live again.

— *Stanley Harrison*

Timely Writer
The Horse Who Started It All

By Kimberly Gatto

imely Writer was a horse who deserved the best of everything. A stunning colt with incredible courage, he was destined for immortality in the world of Thoroughbred racing. The horse was owned by two brothers from the Boston area, where I grew up.

Since he got his start at Suffolk Downs, Timely Writer's name and photos often appeared in the local papers and on the news. I was a young girl, a newcomer to the world of horses and happy to immerse myself in anything horse-related. It was no surprise that I became enamored with this handsome "local hero."

Some people say that great Thoroughbreds have "the look of eagles." It's an elusive trait, and if you ask 10 people to tell you what it means, you'll get 10 different answers. To me, Timely Writer had this quality, which was reflected in his chiseled face and commanding, dark brown eyes. His legs were long and elegant, like a dancer's, and his bay coat gleamed in the sunlight. To my youthful eyes, this horse was nobility.

I was not the only one enamored with Timely Writer. He was a favorite in racing circles as well. Just 3 years old, he had already won 9 races, including key wins in the Champagne Cup and the Florida Derby. While a severe bout of colic had caused him to miss the Kentucky Derby, he had recovered well. His next race would be in the prestigious Jockey Club Gold Cup.

I remember that morning—October 9, 1982. Sitting in the tack room at our barn, I listened as my instructor and another boarder —an old man in a straw hat—marveled at Timely Writer's accomplishments. The old man had strong ties to racing. He pointed out that the Gold Cup was at Belmont Park, the same racetrack where Secretariat and Man o' War had made their marks. I didn't know much about racing, but I knew what it meant to have Timely Writer's name mentioned in the same sentence as two of the sport's greatest horses.

Someone had brought a television to the barn, and we all squeezed into the tack room to watch the race. One of my friends showed me a scrapbook of newspaper clippings and photographs of Timely Writer that she had assembled. As we flipped through the pages, I thought to myself, "This horse is everyone's hero."

Timely Writer went into the starting gate like a champion, dignified and radiating class. When the gates opened, he roared towards the front of the pack. The fans went wild in the stands, cheering as this image of beauty and power ate up the furlongs, running not just for victory, but for the sheer glory of the sport.

Yet fate had something else in mind that day.

Coming around a turn, Timely Writer was what racing people call "bunched up." He and three other horses, all chasing victory, were packed close together through the turn. In a second that seemed like forever, the horses collided and at least two of them fell—but which ones? Where was Timely Writer?

In a split second it became clear that the gallant horse was in trouble, that he had shattered his left front leg. Any other horse would have been stopped by the pain and the shock of the injury, yet Timely Writer's great heart would not give up. Lathered in sweat, blood and grime, he thrashed on the ground in an effort to rise. I stood helpless, watching in horror as the television panned the grisly scene. My mind repeated over and over, "This wasn't supposed to happen. Not to a horse—not to Timely Writer."

Two horses died that day. One was a handsome colt named Johnny Dance; the other, my favorite, Timely Writer.

I never met Timely Writer. I never saw him in person. But I knew everything about him and in a sense he was "my" horse. I was as proud of him as if I owned him. The memory of "my" Timely Writer and his all-too-brief life would impact me forever. Never before had I seen such heart and generosity of spirit from an animal that had unselfishly done what was asked of him, and lost his life in the process. This horse, like many others, had paid the ultimate price to humankind.

Timely Writer was buried at Belmont Park, an honor previously bestowed on another young horse whose life was cut short by a tragic injury. The celebrated filly, Ruffian, had died the same way seven years earlier. Like her, Timely Writer would live on, frozen in time, as a 3 year old destined for stardom.

I will never forget that day or the sadness I felt at the death of that beautiful and vibrant horse. Twenty-two years after his passing, Timely Writer's legacy remains in my heart. His era marked the beginning of my love affair with the Thoroughbred—to me the most soulful and beautiful creature on earth.

Not all Thoroughbreds have the look of eagles, whatever that may mean. Yet when I look into the eyes of a Thoroughbred, I always see the great heart of Timely Writer. I never had the chance to meet this horse that touched me so deeply so many years ago, and he'll never know the impact his life had on mine. But each day I thank God for these wondrous animals that enrich our lives in so many ways.   ៅ

PROLOGUE

A few weeks ago, I was reading a local newspaper when something caught my eye. A mother had written a letter to the advice column asking for suggestions on how to deal with her young daughter, "Kate." The girl had recently lost her beloved horse to colic and, according to the mother, had been acting "strange" ever since. Kate had lost all interest in her schoolwork and friends, was losing weight rapidly and woke up frequently during the night. The mother explained that she and her husband "could not understand" what was wrong with Kate, because it was "only a horse" that had died. Worse yet, when the parents offered to buy her "a better horse," Kate burst into tears and ran to her room, slamming the door behind her.

Fortunately, the writer of the advice column was familiar with grief counseling. He told the girl's mother that the loss of a horse is, to many of us, no different than the death of a human friend or family member. He explained that Kate would likely experience symptoms of grief for days, weeks or even months. She would go through several stages, including guilt, denial, anger and depression, before resigning herself to the loss. Only Kate could determine when she would be ready to accept another horse into her life. Once Kate's parents understood this, he continued, they would be better able to help their daughter heal from her loss.

In recent years, society has begun to recognize the validity and, some might say, the necessity of mourning for a pet. Support groups, Web sites, sympathy cards and books are available to help people cope with pet loss—particularly the death of a small animal such as a dog or cat. Despite these advances, the loss of a horse is often not taken seriously enough.

As owners and riders, we experience a variety of emotions at the loss of a horse. We may wonder if we made the right decision in euthanizing an ailing animal, or we may berate ourselves for not being there when a fatal accident or illness occurred. We may ask ourselves why we missed subtle signs of illness or injury, or whether we did everything we could to prolong the animal's life.

If euthanasia is warranted, additional factors may come into play. While our veterinarians can provide support, the decision to end a horse's suffering is ultimately our own. The situation is different for each individual. Some owners may wish to be with their horse as he or she passes on, while others prefer to remember the horse alive and well.

Our pain does not end with the horse's death. Horses are large animals and deciding where, and how, to handle their remains is a complicated, often painful process in itself.

Losing one horse may lead to increased concern for any remaining horses, and we may panic that something may happen to them. We may feel helpless as a surviving animal grieves for his or her friend. It is important to realize that all of these reactions are normal and that processing them takes time.

Finally, after losing a special equine friend, we may wonder when —and if—we will ever love another horse. We may question whether the horse that died would "approve" of a new mount, or we may simply not want to risk being hurt again. For some, the healing process may take years, while others may choose to welcome a new horse into their lives immediately.

While death causes the most common form of bereavement, equestrians may also suffer grief from losing a horse through other circumstances. Some owners may be forced to sell a much-loved horse due to finances, moving away, outgrowing the animal, unsuitability or going off to college. Other situations, such as giving up a horse at the end of a lease or donating the animal to a retirement farm, may also cause us to grieve.

Following the loss of a horse, well-wishers who do not understand the human-equine bond may tell us that "it's just a horse" or to "get another one." They may urge us to "snap out of it" or "move on." This only makes us feel misunderstood and alone in our grief.

The process of writing this book was not an easy one. Listening to the stories of others and formatting them for this book was upsetting at times. As horse owners, we know how precious our horses are to us and we could easily relate—sometimes too easily—to the stories we were told. They became real to us, and difficult to clear from our minds. We had enough material to fill multiple books and found it challenging to select certain excerpts and not others. Finally, we wondered if the horse world was ready for a book like this.

Beyond the Rainbow Bridge is designed to help equestrians (and those close to them) understand, cope with and, eventually, heal from, the loss of a horse. Equestrians from all walks of life—from backyard riders to international competitors—share a common bond when it comes to loss. It is our hope that their stories and practical advice will provide comfort in your journey through the healing process. ⌁

PART I

The Loss of a Horse

God saw he was getting tired, and a cure was not to be.
So He put His arms around him and whispered, "Come with me."
With tearful eyes we watched him suffer and slowly fade away.
Although we loved him dearly, we could not make him stay.
A golden heart stopped beating; graceful hooves were put to rest.
God broke our hearts to prove to us, He only takes the best.

— Anonymous

CHAPTER 1

SoBo's Story

By Doris Worcester, MSW, LICSW

SoBo (short for He's So Bold) was a 15-year-old chestnut gelding with a star, a snip, a strip and four white socks. He was five months into a year-long layup after an injury to the deep digital flexor tendon in his right hind leg. SoBo was diagnosed at that time with mechanical founder, a gradual stretching of the sensitive laminae of the foot. Not long after, it appeared that he was beginning to develop a "sinker." (As the laminae tear, they can no longer support the coffin bone, which then rotates and moves toward the sole of the foot, hence the term "sinker.") With a case of founder this severe, the hoof wall separates at the coronary band, and it is possible for the entire hoof capsule to slough off. In a sense, a horse could literally step right out of its hoof.

At that time in veterinary medicine, no horse had ever survived this problem. Maureen van der Stad, his owner, was doing everything possible to keep SoBo comfortable, as there was always the possibility that the separation would not be complete.

On a Tuesday in November, it appeared that the separation was worsening and SoBo was in a great deal of pain. It became clear that the pain medication he was receiving was no longer helping him. Extremely high doses of medication would only help for 15 minutes when the effect should have lasted for hours. Maureen slept in the barn with SoBo that night in order to be there if he needed her. She also wanted to spend as much time as possible with him so she could be clear in her own mind and heart exactly what it was that she was asking him to endure. At the time, even the equine hospitals would not accept a horse with an active separation at the coronary band.

Spending all that time with SoBo helped Maureen realize that saying goodbye to him was not about giving up but rather it was the best gift she could give to her beloved horse. She talked to him during her night in the barn and told SoBo that if he were not any better by the following day, she would help him leave his body.

By mid-morning on Wednesday, Maureen had no doubt that letting him go was the best thing she could do for SoBo. After making her decision, Maureen followed an impulse to take photographs of their last hours together, which really helped her. Later, Maureen was able to look back at the photos and realize that she had not imagined the look in SoBo's eye or the tension in his body from enduring so much pain.

Maureen spent almost all of this time alone with SoBo, creating a deep bond of closeness. The self timer on the camera captured some very sweet, tender moments between them, which helped Maureen see that SoBo had some comfort in his final hours.

SoBo had endured a lot, and it showed on his body. Maureen began to prepare him for the afterlife so he would look his best and feel proud. She got out her enormous grooming kit with all his favorite brushes and proceeded with the long version of her grooming ritual. She rubbed aromatic oils on him in a way similar to the ancient human ritual of anointing loved ones in preparation for burial. She found this very comforting. Maureen talked to SoBo as she groomed him, which helped solidify in her mind the reason she made the decision to help him leave his body. She also explained to him what was going to occur, how it was going to happen and who would help him.

Maureen braided a long piece of SoBo's tail and cut the braid off so she would have a piece of him always. She then took an inconspicuous piece of her own hair and braided it into SoBo's mane so that he could be buried with it and take a part of Maureen with him as he left this life. Maureen talked to him about everything that was happening and this gave them both an opportunity to be there for each other. SoBo seemed to understand. He nuzzled Maureen's back all the way up her spine and then gave her face a lick.

Maureen's grandfather had been a horseman, and she said a prayer asking him to greet SoBo on the other side and "claim" him as a family member—but also told him not to be too surprised if SoBo chose to go his own way and run free with his ancestors.

SoBo looked stunning after his grooming ritual, just like the healthy, vibrant horse he used to be. Maureen led his barn mate, Larry, out into the aisle with SoBo where they could share the same hay net and spend some time alone together to say their goodbyes. Maureen went in to call the vet and tell him, "This is the day."

When the vet arrived, Maureen asked him to give SoBo a double dose of relaxants since he had a high tolerance for medication and she wanted the process to go as smoothly as possible. The vet spoke with Maureen again about her decision. It helped because Maureen didn't feel as if they were rushing anything. Maureen's husband, Chris, came home from work to be with her, and the barn owners, her neighbors, were there also. They all helped when needed, but gave Maureen and SoBo space to be alone and say goodbye.

Earlier that day, Maureen had chosen the perfect spot for SoBo's burial on land that could never be developed. When it came time to walk out, SoBo had to have his leg nerve-blocked because he had great difficulty walking on his foundered foot. Everyone was patient and supportive of him. SoBo's barn mate, Larry, was walked out also so that he could have a companion and friend with him. After they arrived at the spot, everyone had a last moment to say goodbye to SoBo while Maureen held the lead rope. The vet allowed Maureen all the time she needed to say her own goodbyes, and she felt complete with her decision, knowing there was nothing left unsaid between her and SoBo.

After the lethal dose was administered, SoBo hit the ground hard and slipped right out of his halter. Everyone rushed to him on the ground. But Maureen had the thought that he was leaving this life as he had entered—free and unrestrained, just the way she wanted him to be buried. Even though SoBo's body was there, Maureen felt that his spirit had already gone before he went down. Maureen knew without question that he had been ready to leave this life.

Maureen was able to spend some time there with his body, which was very helpful to her. She touched and stroked SoBo, admiring how beautiful he was. She cried on his shoulder and examined the hoof in question, seeing quite clearly that the coffin bone was beginning to break through the sole of his foot. And for a while, she simply sat with him.

During this time, her neighbor asked the backhoe driver to "prepare the site." This was how Maureen thought of it—"preparing the site" rather than "digging the hole." When the site was ready, Maureen went back to the barn with her husband as SoBo's body was buried. Her neighbors called back to her after his body was placed in the ground, and everyone admired this beautiful horse one last time. The backhoe driver treated SoBo's body with great care and respect, which was very helpful. He told Maureen that his wife had raised Quarter Horses and he had buried quite a few horses in the past. He added that he had never seen a horse put down with such love and respect, and that he was quite moved.

When it felt right, everyone threw a handful of dirt around SoBo, and the backhoe driver filled in the hole.

Maureen's neighbor had to leave right after SoBo's burial to pick up another horse to be the new companion for her horse Larry after SoBo's death. Larry had a difficult time being alone. Maureen stayed with Larry, and that helped her feel she was not leaving right away and abandoning SoBo. During her wait, Maureen made sure she could identify the burial site so she could find it in the future, and she once again took a picture of where SoBo was interred. As she waited, she brushed Larry and shared her grief with him.

When Maureen went home, she could feel SoBo's presence. It seemed to loom really big and high over the trees around her house. That felt nice for Maureen, and she fell into a deep sleep that evening.

The next day was extremely difficult for Maureen. SoBo had taken up such a big space in her life, and now there was such a gaping emptiness. She listened to a Penelope Smith tape called "On Animal Death and Dying." She folded her laundry and cried a lot. Maureen felt happy that SoBo's ordeal was over yet sad that her dear friend was gone.

Maureen decided to put SoBo's tail braid in a special wooden box with his picture on top, along with some other personal things that were his. On Friday of that week she went out and sprinkled blue corn under a tree as a gift to the earth that held his body. She hung up some Tibetan prayer flags, appropriately called "Windhorses," to help ease and honor his transition. (In the Tibetan tradition, prayer flags contain prayers or blessings. They are hung outdoors where the wind can activate their blessings for happiness, peace, enlightenment and protection.)

Maureen's golden retriever, Sunny, was with her as she sprinkled the corn. And she sat under the tree with Sunny and cried.

Eventually, when Maureen felt it was right, she took down the prayer flags and placed them in a covered box. After SoBo's death, people who knew both him and Maureen became aware of his passing and sent cards, notes and even flowers. Maureen had believed she would only upset someone by sending him or her a card about the loss of an animal, but she was wrong. It helped her to know that people were truly touched by SoBo's life. Maureen saved all these cards and remembrances in her box with the prayer flags, and she looks at them when she wants to connect with SoBo and the people who loved him.

That Saturday, Maureen agreed to help out her friend at the barn where SoBo was buried, and she found that being alone there, feeling all her emotions, was helpful. She hadn't moved any of his things out of the barn yet, so she did it then, in peace and quiet and in the presence of

SoBo's spirit. Maureen then went out to his grave feeling so grateful that the place where SoBo rests can never be developed, and she sprinkled blue corn around his burial site.

Over the next few weeks, Maureen searched for a photo box in which to put all of SoBo's pictures as a tribute. She had the film developed of their last times together, of SoBo's burial site and of the prayer flags. Maureen took her time putting the picture box together, remembering their life together, how much she loved SoBo and what a good friend he had been. She has kept all of those mementos and it has allowed her to feel SoBo's presence to this day.

Maureen had kept SoBo's leg wraps, unwashed, in a bag for more than a year. The unwashed wraps helped her feel she was not rushing him out of her life. For a long time the wraps smelled like SoBo, and Maureen took great comfort in that. As a final tribute, when the time felt right, Maureen ceremoniously washed SoBo's leg wraps, rolled them up neatly and placed them with her keepsakes. ◜

CHAPTER 2

The Grieving Process

By Doris Worcester, MSW, LICSW

The loss of a horse, whether through death, sale or other circumstances, can be a powerful and overwhelming experience. The horse-human relationship is a unique bond—horses can be our friends, our teachers, our challenges. How you grieve your loss will be personal, and the bereavement process will be influenced by many factors: the nature of your relationship with your horse, the length of time you were together, your age, your horse's age, the circumstances surrounding the loss (sudden death or euthanasia, retirement, sale), the meaning and significance you ascribe to the relationship, cultural norms and your personal beliefs about death. All of these factors will play some role in how you will experience grief and resolve your loss.

My clinical training taught me that there are several stages of grief—shock, denial, guilt, anger, fear, bargaining, depression and, finally, acceptance. My treatment experience has shown me that these stages can be fluid and reoccur—that grieving is not a linear process. You may find yourself experiencing a multitude of feelings and thoughts that ebb and flow over time. There is no "right way" to grieve.

Although there is no set formula for grieving, it can be helpful to recognize and understand the common characteristics of bereavement. It is also helpful to know that grieving can begin well before the actual loss of your horse as a form of anticipatory mourning. It is much the same process.

Stages of Grief

Shock

Initially, the death of a beloved companion may be experienced as a state of shock—you may feel numb, bewildered and confused. Things may feel unreal and time may seem distorted. You may feel weak, have a loss of appetite, have difficulty sleeping or sleep too much. You may have vivid dreams of your horse and perhaps even feel or see his or her presence. All of these reactions are normal.

Kat Hampton, a lifelong rider, describes her feelings after the death of her horse, Cautious Val, who fractured his leg in a paddock accident:

I sat staring blankly at the computer screen for what seemed like an eternity. Val's death, so sudden and unexpected, did not seem real. He was my best equine friend and, in an instant, he was gone. Even worse, I hadn't been able to say goodbye.

My husband knew that I needed some time alone and took our young son out for the afternoon. After they left, I typed a post on my favorite online equine message board, letting everyone know that Val was free from pain, galloping in green meadows across the Rainbow Bridge. As comforting as it was to have the support and sympathies of my online friends, I kept returning to posts that had been made before Val died. It was just too much to accept that he was gone forever.

Anger

It is also normal to feel other emotions, some of which may surprise you. You may begin to feel intense anger, often accompanied by guilt or fear. You may blame yourself for things you wished you had or had not done. You may blame others for things you felt they should or should not have done. If you believe in a higher power, you may be angry at God for depriving you of your beloved companion. You may even feel angry at your horse for leaving you and for the feelings you are experiencing after his or her death.

Fear

You may also feel increased anxiety, even panic, as you enter this unknown and unfamiliar experience of loss. You may worry about the future loss of another horse or about something equally catastrophic happening. Your sense of vulnerability in general may increase. You may feel disillusioned, disoriented and disenchanted as you ask the question, "How could this happen to me?" Your basic assumptions about the world and your secure place in it may be temporarily challenged.

Bargaining

If you are anticipating the loss of your horse, you may engage in the process of "bargaining"—asking God (and perhaps even your veterinarian) to forestall or prevent your horse's death in exchange for your willingness to change your life in some way. You may secretly promise many things for the possibility of saving your horse's life.

Depression

Following the loss, you may experience a period of intense sadness, accompanied by feelings of helplessness, hopelessness and despair. The impulse to withdraw and isolate yourself may be strong. You may not want to visit the barn and face the empty stall where your horse once lived. In fact, you may wish to avoid horses altogether for a while. This is normal—it is nature's way of promoting healing. You may also find yourself yearning deeply for your horse and having difficulty imagining a life without him or her. You may begin to remember and grieve anew other losses from the past. Your concentration and focus may be noticeably impaired until your depression lifts. Making decisions and remembering details may become difficult.

Kat Hampton recalls:

> *Though my heart wasn't in it, I found myself putting on my shoes and walking outside to the horse pasture. There I stood, staring at my remaining herd of five, wondering if I would ever share with them the strong connection I had with Val. I had no desire to ride or even be with any of the horses that afternoon, but felt as if I needed to be there. I was afraid that if I didn't force myself to be with a horse that day, I might never be able to love another.*

Acceptance

Eventually, you will experience a sense of reorganization and integration around your loss as you move toward acceptance. You will begin to feel stronger and more energized, and you will start reconnecting with familiar people, places and things, particularly in your experiences with horses. You may find yourself wanting to bring a new horse into your life, or simply reconnect with those that are already there for you. The loss of your horse will have new meaning, and your heart can now open to the possibility of a new bond with another companion.

What to Do Following Your Loss

Remember, there is no right or wrong way to mourn. It is important to simply accept what you are thinking and feeling moment to moment without judgment. Keep in mind that grief is a transitional process of moving between an ending and a beginning—from one state of certainty to another. It is a personal and unique process of adaptation and adjustment, with its own sense of timing and pacing.

In many ways our culture does not value or validate the significance and meaning of the loss of a horse. You may subtly (or not so subtly) be encouraged to "get over it" by your friends, relatives and acquaintances. "After all, it was only a horse … " they may say. You may feel alone and isolated with your experience and attempt to hide your feelings. Try to be willing to acknowledge and express your feelings when they arise. Associate with people who will listen and accept your thoughts and feelings and will not ask you to inhibit them because of their own discomfort. Talk about your loss with people only if and when it feels right for you.

Tune into both your body and mind. In an ongoing fashion, quiet yourself and ask the body-mind: "What would help me with this loss right now?" "How do I want to say goodbye?" "What will help me stay connected to my beloved horse after death?" The body-mind will answer through thoughts, images, body sensations, energy movements and feelings. Only you will know what is right and aligned for yourself at this time. Learn to open this channel of knowing more fully through meditation, breathing or prayer using the whole self—body-mind-spirit—to aid in the resolution of your grief.

In a practical sense, there are many things that you can do that may help you with your loss. In the beginning you may want to leave your horse's stall empty as a tribute and acknowledgement of his or her life. This may help you feel that you are not rushing yourself through the grieving process, and it may provide the comfort of being with your horse's spirit or energy presence even though his or her physical body is gone.

You may want to create some rituals to support and guide you through the mourning process. This will help make your loss more real, allow you to know and express your thoughts and feelings, ground and center you, and help you connect to your beloved friend in a clear and conscious way.

One ritual might be the creation of a funeral or memorial ceremony at or around the time of your horse's death. This may include other people who were connected to and loved your horse, or it may be a solitary rite.

You might write a letter to your horse acknowledging your love and thanking the horse for his or her friendship. You might write a story about your life together, highlighting what was special about your horse's personality and your relationship. You can create a visual memorial: a collage, scrapbook or album of photographs, objects or symbols of your horse that you can revisit over time.

You may wish to save something from your horse that is precious and has meaning for you—a halter, leg wraps, a lock of mane or tail, a horseshoe or nail, or an article of clothing. If your horse's death is not sudden but anticipated, you might want to create a video or photo history of him or her now to help you stay connected through the mourning process after he or she is gone. You could also create a living memorial by planting a tree or garden or create a static memorial by placing a structure, statue, totem or symbolic object in a spot where you can visit, reflect and meditate whenever you want.

Perhaps you would like to create a "dance stick" as a lasting connection to your horse as the Lakota warriors did. To the Lakota, a horse was a trusted friend on whom he relied in battle, in hunting, and for transportation. When a horse died, the warrior would fashion a dance stick in his or her memory by attaching a piece of the horse's mane, along with beads, feathers, and other symbolic items and carry the stick in ceremony to honor the horse's life. You can create a medicine bundle of special items related to your horse and attach it to your dance stick.

You may want to create an indoor memorial—a place for special reflection and connection with your horse. On a table or shelf you can display a picture or pictures of your horse together with meaningful and symbolic items associated with him or her. You can light a candle, burn incense, sage or lemongrass, play music or sing. You can use this special place as a way to open your mind and spirit and connect to the soul and presence of your friend.

You may wish to volunteer or perform service in an equine-related organization or donate to a horse-related charity as a tribute to your horse and as a commitment to improving conditions for horses still living.

You may use the experience of loss to find or create more meaning in your own life by going on a retreat or vision quest. Many indigenous cultures organize these formal passage journeys to help guide an individual through difficult or painful life transitions. Often, there is a strengthening of the self and the spirit following such a quest. The death of your horse then serves a higher and greater purpose and is an acknowledgement of the spiritual aspect of your relationship together.

On a day-to-day basis, take good care of yourself. Rest, eat as well as you can, and exercise when you are ready. Create times to be alone and times to be connected. Give yourself opportunities to feel your emotions and to talk about your experience with others. Join a support group or consider counseling. Take time off from work if it feels right for you. Create a journal. Read good information about death, dying and the grieving process—knowledge will help you feel less vulnerable and more in control. Don't be afraid to follow your impulses: sing, dance, walk, jump, skip, draw, write, complain, meditate, sleep, cry, laugh or pray.

Above all, give yourself permission to "do nothing" if that is all you feel like doing. Grief is a natural process that cannot be hurried along or shortened—resting and "being" is as essential as activity and "doing." Remind yourself often of this natural pulsation.

Conclusion

In the final analysis, death is inseparable from life. In certain cultures, there is a certainty in the interconnectedness and immortality of all things. Life and death are simply a part of the wholeness and fabric of the infinite universe. Each is a reflection of the other and of a perfect and higher order. You may have your own spiritual philosophy; if so, let it help and inspire you through this transition. Above all, remind yourself that both death and life are miracles—that at the very moment that your horse has died, somewhere a foal is born. ✍

CHAPTER 3

A Consolation

By Nancy Pemberton

y sweet, quirky Seger was gone—put down in December after a month of incessant colics that the vets could neither diagnose nor fix. Since his death, I had become hyper-vigilant with regard to Tommy, my surviving horse, and little Twee, the pony given to us for Christmas. My paranoia was obvious even to my neighbors. I left all of the barn lights on around the clock so I could check on the horses in the middle of my sleepless nights. I agonized over simple things that had never worried me before, called the clinic over trivial problems and refused to be off the property for more than a few hours at a time. And so, that morning when I heard the sound of a horse screaming—Tommy, his whinny sharp, excited—I grabbed my boots and cell phone and bolted for the door.

All the way down to the paddocks, I chanted under my breath the usual mantra: Be on four feet, just be on four feet.

When I got there, Tommy was fine. He was standing at the fence line, staring across the street into my neighbor's field. I hurried over to him and patted his tense, upright neck. He swung his head once in my direction to warn me off, then ignored me, continuing to stare, continuing to scream.

"What is it, buddy? Are you OK?" I asked, and turned my head to see what he was looking at. And then I knew.

My neighbor had acquired a new horse—an elegant brown Thoroughbred that grazed quietly near the farthest gate. He was clothed in the same kind of rug my own horses wore. All you could see were his dark head and faded muzzle, his neck and long, fine legs. I saw a hint of white on the heel of one hind foot. From where Tommy and I stood, he looked exactly like Seger.

My heart skipped a beat, and for one fleeting second, I thought I saw what Tommy saw. Seger, not in the right pasture, but standing there nonetheless. Tommy couldn't have known Seger's destination when he left that fateful morning three weeks before. Tommy had seen Seger leave the farm and come back many times. For all he knew, Seger had simply gone to another horse show, from which he would eventually return. And so he called again to this horse, not with a shrill whinny this time, but with the soft, inviting mutter of one old friend to another.

"It's not Seger," I said, and Tommy's ears flickered at the name. The tears that were never far away these days filled my eyes. Caught up in my own grieving, I had failed to properly assess or value how Tommy was processing all of this.

I walked to the barn and got some hay, a flake of bright alfalfa to draw Tommy away from the fence line and the horse that wasn't Seger. He trotted over willingly enough, but dragged as much of the hay as he could manage back to the fence so he could eat and keep an eye on his old friend. It wouldn't seem that odd or bothersome to him that Seger was living across the street now; they had been separated by greater distances at boarding barns in the past, and he had the pony for company at any rate. Seger was back in his life, and that was all that mattered.

I walked to where he stood and pushed my face into his thick mane, sick of tears and mourning. With Seger restored to him, Tommy no longer needed my pity or my company, and as if to make that clear, he stepped away from me and dropped his head to eat. I turned to look again at the horse across the street, the horse that was not Seger. I searched

for differences, rejecting the irrational hope that said that miracles happen, that somehow Seger had not died. Behind me, Tommy snorted in the way that horses do only when they are at their most content. Gripped by sudden envy, I tugged at his forelock and forced him to look at me. "It's not him," I insisted again, and Tommy pulled away.

What would it hurt, I wondered, to believe, like Tommy, that the Thoroughbred we watched was indeed Seger? Philosopher Roger Scruton wrote, "The consolation of imaginary things is not imaginary consolation," and surely that is true. Something that felt like peace settled over me, nudging aside the grief that had lodged for so long inside of me. I leaned with Tommy against the fence and said, in a voice too low to carry across the street, "Hey, Sege." The horse looked up abruptly and my heart gave again that funny leap. Then my eyes fell to his white heel and I laughed out loud—the markings were on the wrong foot.

That was enough. Seger was dead and would not be coming back. But he was at peace, and so was Tommy and so was I. It was time for me to go back to the house and back to my life and to take consolation from the horses that remained.

Still, as I trudged across the pasture through the snow, I decided I would avoid my neighbor for the next few days. I didn't want to talk about her new horse quite yet; just for a little while, I didn't want to learn his name. ⮌

CHAPTER 4

Coping with Sudden Loss

The sudden loss of a horse is a catastrophic event that changes our lives forever. Sudden losses come in many forms. It may be an accident, barn fire or illness that occurs with no warning, and with no time to save the horse. Owners have lost horses to colic and other rapid-onset illnesses. Some barn managers have had the horrible experience of finding a horse dead or fatally injured in its stall or paddock. Others may be riding a horse when it suddenly breaks down. In a split second, the world changes and, after a sudden loss, nothing will ever be the same.

Fourteen-year-old Kaylie Chaffee recalls being told that Luka, the horse she'd ridden and shown for three years, was fatally injured:

> *On a rainy August 21, I was away from the barn at my uncle's wedding. My mom received a phone call and told me to come out to the car with her. I had no idea what was going on or why I was going, but I followed her anyway. My mom then told me that Luka had been kicked*

and her leg was badly broken; there was no way to save her. As soon as I heard those words, tears began pouring from my eyes.

When we pulled up to the farm, my heart stopped for a second. I couldn't see where anyone was because there were so many cars blocking my view. As I stepped out of the car, one of my instructors ran toward me, waving her hands and telling me to stop. She approached me, drenched with rain and tears, and said, "She went down quietly." All of a sudden I felt weak and helpless. For the first time in my life I couldn't hold back from crying or keep myself under control. I fell into my instructor's arms and began crying harder than I ever had before.

After the Loss

For the first few days after a sudden loss, you may find yourself pretending or hoping that it was all "just a bad dream." You may forget that your horse is gone, and you may set out grain and hay for him simply out of habit. You may imagine that you see him or hear him whinny. These are all normal ways in which the human mind grapples with the shock of sudden loss.

If the horse has died as the result of an illness or injury, you may begin second guessing yourself. Thoughts such as, "Why did I let him outside in that icy paddock?" or "I should have known that horse would kick him!" may race through your mind. "What ifs" may keep you awake at night. If you were away at the time of the accident or illness, you may wonder if things would have been different if you'd stayed home. As troubling as such thoughts may be, they are a natural part of the grieving process. Sadly, accidents and illnesses occur no matter how careful we are.

Saying Goodbye

One of the most difficult aspects of sudden loss is that we typically do not have the opportunity to say goodbye. Viewing a body is one way to have "closure," which is why some religions offer "wakes" or "viewings" when a human being dies. If at all possible, you may wish to take the opportunity to spend time with the horse's body in order to accept the finality of its death. This is a matter of individual preference. Some people may opt to remember the horse alive and well.

Kaylie Chaffee recalls the moments after Luka's passing:

They asked me if I wanted to see her—there was no doubt that I did. As I walked over, the tears just kept coming. When I saw Luka's body just lying there, the worst feeling came over me—a feeling I cannot even explain. As I got closer, everyone was watching me. Luka's owner (my instructor) gave me a big hug, and we cried together. After that, everyone told me they were sorry, and the vet said that it was the best decision to put Luka down. I know everyone there meant well, but as every horseperson knows, putting your horse down never seems like the best thing to do at the time. All of my barn friends let me have my alone time with Luka so that I could say goodbye. I sat with her for a long time, and all the while, I never stopped crying.

Sadly, in some instances, saying goodbye in such a way is not possible. Kat Hampton was not able to be with her Val when he passed away:

As I struggled to dress myself, the vet called. He described Val's fracture as a "catastrophic injury" and told me that nothing further could be done to save my beloved horse. I told the vet that while I had wanted to be there to comfort my horse in his passing, I could not bear to let him suffer for the time it would take for us to get there. He would have my permission to end Val's suffering immediately. Within half an hour I received the call that Val was no longer in pain.

The following Sunday, my husband and I drove out to the farm to see where they had buried Val. I found it very touching that the barn own-

ers had placed flowers on his gravesite. They asked if I wanted to sit by Val's grave and be alone for a while, but I didn't need to. I only wanted to see the grave to get the closure I so desperately needed.

Death of a Friend's Horse

You may experience the pain of a sudden loss even if it is not your own horse. The death of a barn mate—or even a horse you did not know personally—in a sudden and/or violent manner may remind you of your own horse's mortality. Kimberly Gatto recalls her feelings at the tragic loss of a friend's horse:

> *When I arrived at the barn, my trainer took me aside and told me that my friend Gail's mare had fractured her leg in the paddock that morning and had to be euthanized. She had already been buried out back. It was all so shocking and sudden to me—we'd just ridden together the day before!*
>
> *I was determined to be strong for my friend, so I kept my feelings of grief inside. A week later, as my mom was driving me to school, I broke down in tears. Not only was I shocked and upset by my friend's sudden loss, but I was plagued with anxiety that the same fate would befall my own mare. I was 18 and had just lost my father to a heart attack, so the thought of another sudden loss was just too much for me to bear.*

The Famous Horse

Similar feelings can arise at the sudden death of a famous horse. Like human celebrities, horses at the top of their sport can become icons to us, and their deaths can impact us on a personal level. Thousands mourned the recent death of Chris Kappler's 2004 Olympic mount, Royal Kaliber. People often recall their heartbreak at the racing deaths of

Ruffian and Go for Wand. Ruffian's loss was especially difficult for racing fans of all ages. Lisa Carusone writes:

I was 12 years old when Ruffian died on July 6, 1975. Even though I was young, I had the unmistakable sense that the world was changing for women. I also knew that this change would not come easily and that, at that time, women couldn't just be accomplished in their own right. They had to be better than men and able to beat them at their own game. I still don't know whose idea it was to pit Ruffian, the best filly of her class, against Foolish Pleasure, that year's Kentucky Derby winner. He was great and so was she; that should have been the end of it. To me, this race, more than any other I've watched, took on a meaning that went far beyond the confines of racing. Each of these horses carried the extra weight of a society trying to sort itself out. It co-opted a champion filly and cost a beautiful horse her life.

For equine photographer John Bellucci, Ruffian's loss was even more personal:

I got to see her at her barn in the mornings, watch her work and get bathed and cooled out afterward.

The track that day was like a festival, but later, of course, everything changed. When I discovered she'd broken down, I raced out across the infield with some other people. By the time we got to the other side, Doc Gillman already had the cast on her leg, and the horse ambulance was coming around the turn. There was so much blood ... it filled the air cast.

I was among the group of people who waited outside Dr. Reed's hospital the night of the surgery, and we all knew when Ruffian woke up. It sounded like a war was going on in there. I was at the burial later that evening. The memory is as fresh today, as though it just happened.

A sudden loss can be particularly devastating since, in many instances, the horse is young and dies "before its time." We wonder what could have been had the animal lived into its prime. We may wonder, for example, if Ruffian's progeny would have inherited her gallant spirit, or what Royal Kaliber may have accomplished in the years to come. The sudden death of any horse, young and vibrant or older and more frail, reminds us of the overall fragility of life and to enjoy each day as it comes.

Necropsy

If your horse has died of sudden, uncertain causes, you may wish to have a necropsy (animal autopsy) performed in order to pinpoint the cause of death. In some cases, this may bring closure to a difficult situation. Trainer Amy Neal chose this option after the unexpected death of her horse, Gerri:

> Gerri was a 13-year-old Arabian gelding who had become a beloved family member. He passed away suddenly in the middle of a winter's night; I found him dead the next morning. I was nine months pregnant at the time and very distraught.
>
> I was not sure what had caused Gerri's death. He had been fine the night before. I had assumed Gerri had colicked and was beating myself up over it, thinking that perhaps I had missed some signs or symptoms. I wanted to know what happened but I was not sure if I could handle the thought of putting Gerri's body through a necropsy. With the help and support of some great friends and boarders, I made the decision to have one performed.
>
> The results of the necropsy showed that Gerri had an aortic aneurysm and it had burst. This knowledge gave me a great amount of relief. There was nothing I could have done to prevent his death. While

nothing would change how I felt in losing Gerri, it was comforting to hear that his death had been quick and painless.

Conclusion

There is an old saying that lightning rarely strikes twice, and then, never in the same place. The challenge of moving on after suddenly losing a horse goes beyond the lost opportunity to say goodbye. The test is in restoring faith in the future, and realizing that it holds ample opportunity for closure and healing. While the experience can never be erased, with time, your recollections of the horse and the wonderful times you shared together will be the memories to which you turn.

PART II

Crossing the Bridge

I stood beside your bed last night, I came to have a peep.
I could see that you were crying, you found it hard to sleep.
I whinnied to you softly as you brushed away a tear,
"It's me, I haven't left you, I'm well, I'm fine, I'm here."

I was with you at my grave today, you tend it with such care.
I want to reassure you, that I'm not lying there.
I walked with you towards the house, as you fumbled for your key.
I put my head against you, nickered and said, "It's me."

You looked so very tired, and sank into a chair.
I tried so hard to let you know that I was standing there.
It's possible for me to be so near you everyday.
To say to you with certainty, "I never went away."

You sat there very quietly, then smiled, I think you knew ...
in the stillness of that evening, I was very close to you.
And when the time is right for you to cross the brief divide,
I'll gallop across to greet you and we'll stand there, side by side.

I have so many things to show you, there's so much for you to see.
Be patient, live your journey out ... then come home to be with me.

— *Author Unknown*

CHAPTER 5

Skippy's Gifts

By Jennifer Shirey

It was once said that, "Every gift from a friend is a wish for your happiness." I learned the truth of those prophetic words on a summer's night four months ago.

Skippy came into my life on a winter's day in early 2002. He was my first horse—bought for me with my own money. A large, pure-white Andalusian, Skippy was the horse I had always dreamed of and longed for. We had some rough spots along our journey, but in the end, I trusted him with my life.

So began our lesson on a beautiful Saturday morning in August 2004. After a summer of working on flying changes, we managed to pull it together and get almost every one just right. I don't recall how many fences we jumped that day, but I do remember that they were good—all of them.

Following our lesson, I cooled out Skippy as usual and put him away to have his breakfast. Midway though his meal, however, he suddenly stopped eating. That was not normal for him, and when he stood in the corner pawing and curling his lip, I knew something wasn't right. We walked a bit, and I called the vet.

Dr. Staten arrived shortly and examined Skippy. The news was not good when she palpated him; things were not where they were supposed to be. We loaded Skippy onto the trailer to take him to the nearby clinic, where it was determined that he needed surgery.

Fortunately, we had caught the colic in its early stages. During surgery, the vets found that the tissue was still pink and viable and simply needed to be "rearranged." The veterinarians were able to save the entire intestinal tract, and Skippy came out of surgery as well as expected. Without complications, he would be coming home within 10 days. Skippy was only 13 years old and in great physical condition, so his prognosis was good. I was hopeful that we'd be the ones to make it through, but knew the vet was still guarded in his prognosis.

On the third day post-surgery, things took a turn for the worse. Skippy spiked a high fever and his GI tract began to shut down. Despite the vets' best efforts, his health continued to fail. On the following day, I could see that things were not getting better. I had hoped so hard that in a few months, I'd be sending the veterinarians and clinic staff a letter and a picture of Skippy to show them how well he was doing. With colic surgery, there are no guarantees, and while 80 percent of the time it is successful, I knew we still had a 20 percent chance to fail. In my mind, I think I knew where we were headed, but in my heart, I still held out some hope.

As I sat with Skippy and thought about what he'd gone through, I decided that my beloved horse had been through enough. The vet had one more drug to try, and we would know fairly quickly whether or not it would help restore Skippy's gut motility. The vet promised that once he could no longer control Skippy's pain, we'd be done.

After receiving this medication, Skippy was comfortable and seemed to be getting some good gut sounds back. But we had yet to see anything pass through the GI tract.

I will never forget that afternoon. Despite being on his feet since his surgery, despite being hungry, sick and not himself, my wonderful horse gave me his very last gift.

That afternoon was not as hot as a typical August day in the

Southwestern desert. Instead, the days were ever so slightly shorter than they are in mid-summer, and the temperature was just slightly better than usual (under 100 degrees). The vet let me take Skippy for a walk behind the barn, on a little trail through the desert. And so we walked, gingerly at first, and then more confidently, around and around in a big circle. Every so often, he would stop and stand and look content and comfortable, if only for a moment. And as the sun set that evening, I was so grateful to still have my beautiful horse with me.

They always say you'll know when it's time to say goodbye, and now I know it's true. The vet did everything he could to keep Skippy comfortable, but shortly before midnight that same night, I received the call that every horse owner dreads: Skippy's pain was beyond anything that medication could help.

When I arrived at the clinic, Skippy was so far from himself. All I could do was hug him, kiss him, pet his ears and stroke his face and tell him that it was ok to go. There was nothing left for him to give. I had asked him to endure so much, truly believing it would help him and trying what we could to save him. What had seemed like a possibility only a few hours earlier slipped away from us, and it was time to set him free from his pain.

No one wants to have to make that final decision and yet, it is the most wonderful gift we can give to the animals we love. I will forever have an empty spot in my heart for Skippy. He exceeded every expectation I had of him and took me beyond my dreams in riding. But with Skippy, it wasn't just about the riding. He was my friend, and it would have been enough just to have had him for himself. To me, it was all about what I could do to make his life meaningful and to keep the connection between us. In his passing, I've made a new friend in his original owner, who was heartbroken to ever let him go and saddened again by his passing. Getting to know her explained so much about why he thrived with me, and it gave me comfort to know how loved and cherished he had been.

Following Skippy's death, I wanted to plant something in his memory, something that could live on when he could not. I believed that doing nothing would simply serve to magnify my grief; I needed something to do. I had nothing specific in mind and went to a nursery near my house to browse. Upon entering the store, the "plant of the month" was the first thing I saw, and it was pretty—light green foliage with small grape-like clusters of purple flowers. Yet I didn't want to pick the first thing I saw and began to walk away. That's when I saw the name of the plant—"Sweet Memory." What could be more perfect than that? I picked out the fullest, healthiest looking plant I could find and added some precious snips of Skippy's tail hair when I planted it in the soil. So far, it's thriving, just as he did and as he now does, free of pain and suffering.   ✒

CHAPTER 6

Euthanasia: A Veterinarian's Perspective

By Jennifer E. King, DVM

hoosing to euthanize a horse is one of the most difficult decisions a horse owner has to make. It is also one of the kindest, and most responsible, decisions we can make for a beloved equine companion during a time of incurable suffering. The word "euthanasia" is derived from the Greek "eu," meaning "good," and "thanatos," meaning "death". We are fortunate that through veterinary science we are able to provide a painless end to an animal's suffering.

In practical terms, a horse owner should consider "quality of life" as the main criteria for choosing euthanasia. Will the horse continue to suffer without hope of living comfortably? Has there been a catastrophic injury, or is there an acute medical condition with a grave prognosis? It is best to fully discuss these questions with your veterinarian. Justification for euthanasia should be based on medical circumstances rather than economic concerns.

The American Association of Equine Practitioners (AAEP) offers its own set of ethical and professional guidelines, which is available on AAEP's Web site, www.myhorsematters.com. According to AAEP, the following criteria should be considered when determining the "necessity for intentional euthanasia of a horse to avoid and terminate incurable and excessive suffering":

☐ *Nature of the illness or injury:* Is the condition chronic and incurable?

☐ *Survival:* Has the condition caused a hopeless prognosis for survival?

☐ *Danger to self or others:* Is the horse a hazard to itself or its handlers?

☐ *Medication:* Will the horse require continuous medication for the relief of pain for the remainder of its life?

Methods of Euthanasia

The most common method of euthanasia utilized in the United States is intravenous injection of a lethal drug. The drug most commonly used is pentobarbital, which is an anesthetic agent. An overdose of the drug is given, which results in a rapid, smooth onset of unconsciousness followed by brain death. This leads to respiratory and cardiac arrest and death in a matter of seconds. A second drug, phenytoin, may also be used in combination. This drug produces cardiac arrest. Because the horse is unconscious, he or she does not feel any pain during the procedure.

If the animal is agitated or difficult to handle, the veterinarian may choose to give a sedative prior to giving the injection of euthanasia solution. He or she may also place an intravenous catheter for the ease of delivering the large volume of medication needed.

An animal may also be euthanized with a single gunshot to the head in a precise location. This is not frequently used in the United State; however, it is a very common method in Europe.

The Process of Euthanasia

In a typical situation, the horse is positioned standing in an open space. The injection is given and within approximately 90 seconds, the animal becomes heavily sedated followed by induction of anesthesia, a state of unconsciousness. The horse may fall abruptly to the ground and may continue to make some movements or even vocalize as the drugs take full effect. The horse will likely take several more deep breaths or sighs. It is not uncommon for the horse to "gasp" or take a few "agonal" breaths (the last respiratory pattern prior to death). There may be muscle tremors or twitches, or even seemingly purposeful movements of the legs. If the animal is recumbent (unable to stand), the process is usually quiet and uneventful, however, the horse may still appear to struggle. The veterinarian will verify that the animal has passed away by confirming cardiac arrest (checking the pulse) and/or checking that the corneal reflex is abolished.

As mentioned previously, it is important to remember that the substance used is an anesthetic agent. While the horse may appear to struggle, he/she is unconscious and does not feel any pain.

Being Present—A Personal Decision

It is a very personal decision whether or not to observe the euthanasia of your horse. Horses are large animals. Unlike the peaceful passing of a dog or cat on a veterinarian's table or in an owner's arms, euthanasia of a horse can be a dramatic and often frightening experience for an owner to witness. We spend so much time and energy keeping our horses on their feet that watching an animal fall during euthanasia can be unsettling; many horse owners are uncomfortable and upset by this sight. Furthermore, it may be a potentially dangerous situation, and limiting the number of people involved is necessary for safety reasons.

Personally, I do not recommend that all of my clients observe the process. I always encourage them to say their personal goodbyes and sometimes even to see the horse after the process is complete. If the euthanasia is planned in advance, it may help to discuss your feelings with friends and family to determine if it would be in your best interest to be present.

Unique Circumstances

There are a few unique circumstances involving euthanasia that should also be addressed. These include: euthanasia of a horse in an owner's absence, unreasonable requests for euthanasia and public health considerations.

A veterinarian may euthanize an animal in the case of a catastrophic emergency (e.g., fractured limb, severe colic or other fatal injury) in an owner's absence. Every attempt is made to contact the owner first; however, the veterinarian can exercise professional judgment and act on the animal's behalf in an absolute emergency.

If a situation arises where it appears as though an animal is suffering inhumanely and the owner has not requested euthanasia, the local SPCA chapter and authorities may become involved.

A veterinarian may refuse to euthanize an animal if he/she believes it is not justified. Examples include an otherwise healthy animal that is pasture sound but not serviceably sound, or an animal that has a good prognosis for recovery with time and treatment.

If there is any concern that the horse has been exposed to or has died from a zoonotic disease (an animal disease that can be spread to humans), it may be necessary to inform local veterinary authorities (such as the local animal control officer or state veterinarian) and to perform a necropsy or other diagnostic tests. For example, if an animal has potentially been exposed to rabies, it is necessary to perform diagnostic tests on brain tissue to confirm or rule out a diagnosis. If the animal is not vaccinated and there has been human or animal exposure, the farm may be quarantined, and post-exposure treatment for the exposed humans may be necessary. While transmission of rabies from horses to humans is exceedingly rare, the situation warrants extreme measures.

Other Considerations

If you have an insurance policy on your horse, the insurance company should be notified as soon as possible of a situation requiring euthanasia. If it is a planned euthanasia, the insurance company should be notified well in advance. Most insurance companies offer a 24-hour service for notification of an emergency illness or injury.

If your horse is insured, you will most likely need to have a complete necropsy in order to place your claim. The fees for necropsy vary depending on what tests are needed.

Owners should check with local authorities to determine if it is legal to bury a horse on private property. There is concern for contamination of ground water or exposing wild animals to drug residues in the carcass. There are other options including pet cemeteries or cremation, which will be discussed in detail in a later section of this book.

Conclusion

It is never easy to say goodbye to a beloved horse. However, when an animal is suffering with no hope for recovery, euthanasia allows us to invoke a peaceful end. It is the final act of kindness we can give to our horses. ❧

CHAPTER 7

Preparing for Goodbye

f your horse is elderly, incurably lame or suffering from a chronic disease, you may find yourself experiencing all the emotions of grief before the horse's actual death. Psychologists call this "anticipatory grief"—mourning that begins before a death actually occurs. The physical and emotional reactions involved are the same as those experienced in normal grieving, as discussed by psychologist Doris Worcester in Chapter 2.

International dressage competitor Cindy Sydnor describes how she grieved for her horse, Lover, who suffered from an incurable neurological disorder:

> *In the weeks before giving the vet permission to euthanize my beloved horse, I allowed myself to mourn for him. It was simply instinctive. I would imagine he was already gone and I was missing him very much. I allowed myself to feel deep sorrow. I did this only when I was completely alone or with Lover in his stall. This was the most painful time for me. I cried a lot and hugged him; he tolerated my behavior very patiently. I was saying goodbye slowly.*

The result of pre-mourning this very dear friend was that by the time he died, I was over the worst of the pain and I did not have to cope with both the fact of his actual death and my pain from the loss all at once. [1]

It is extremely difficult for a caregiver to watch a horse suffer as his or her quality of life deteriorates due to age or illness. You are constantly reminded that your horse will not be around forever and that you may have to make the decision to end the horse's suffering through euthanasia.

Sometimes when a horse requires expensive veterinary treatments and extensive care arrangements, an owner may find him or herself at times hoping that the horse will die on its own. Most owners feel guilty for feeling this way. It is important to realize that this is a normal part of the emotional process of caring for a sick animal, and that thoughts alone have never resulted in the death of a horse. It is simply the mind's way of coping with the impending loss and of relieving the emotional stress and physical strain that comes with caring for a chronically ill horse.

Discussing the Prognosis

While some may find themselves secretly wishing that a terminally ill horse would die, others deny the seriousness and the hopelessness of the horse's condition altogether. They may spend time and money on every type of treatment or surgery available, regardless of the odds of recovery. In these instances, it is important to discuss the horse's prognosis with your veterinarian. If the surgery or treatment will only cause the horse further suffering—without good odds for survival—you may want to reassess the situation. Consider that the treatments may serve to keep the horse alive only for your sake because saying goodbye seems too difficult.

Others cope with the inevitable by "turning a blind eye." They avoid the subject altogether, hoping that the illness will magically disappear or that the horse will miraculously get better. These owners may avoid visiting the horse, tell others and themselves that the horse is "fine," or fail to admit that the horse is ill and unlikely to get better.

Under these circumstances, the owner is not alone in feeling sad and conflicted about the horse's condition. Others in the owner's and horse's circle (veterinarians, farriers, trainers, farm owners, other boarders, family and friends) may also feel the strain of an illness left unacknowledged, despite the horse's visible decline. Kimberly Gatto recalls one such situation from her childhood:

Nelly was a 36 year-old Saddlebred who lived in the stall across from my pony. The mare had been owned by a kind old lady for many, many years. The woman would visit every weekend and mesmerize us kids with stories of the pair's glory days.

Sadly, Nelly's health had deteriorated with old age. Despite being fed almost continuously, her ribs poked visibly through her skin. She was almost totally blind and was confined to her stall because of chronic lameness.

The vet and barn owners gently told the woman that it was past time to end the horse's suffering, but she wouldn't hear of it. She would not allow herself to accept Nelly's plight because, I suppose, it was too painful for her to make that final decision. I think she was hoping the mare would peacefully pass away on her own. Finally, the woman's family convinced her to have Nelly euthanized. It was all so sad. She loved that horse so much, almost too much to let go. I can still picture both of them when I think back to those days. The woman must be gone now, too, and I imagine them together, health restored and happy again.

As Doris Worcester wrote in Chapter 2, you may also engage in the process of "bargaining"—asking God or others to forestall your horse's death in return for your willingness to change your life in some way. You may secretly promise many things to try to save your horse's life. Unfortunately, while perfectly normal to do, such actions only prolongs the inevitable end of your horse's life and may leave you feeling that you've lost your horse because you failed to keep your end of the "bargain," or because your "bargain" was too meager an offering.

Happy Memories

If your horse is likely facing euthanasia, you may choose to use his or her remaining time on earth to plan for what lies ahead and to spend some quality time with your equine friend. Many experts believe that having time to prepare for a death has its positive aspects; we may sort out our feelings, make the remaining time we have with our horse more personally meaningful, make arrangements for burial or cremation and begin planning any memorials ahead of time. During this time, it is important to ensure that your horse is as comfortable as possible and that all of his needs are being met. While it may be easier to distance yourself by staying away from the barn, it is important to remember that your horse depends on you and needs your attention and companionship at this time. Kimberly Gatto writes:

> Rhino's euthanasia was scheduled for a Monday. The week before, my instructor (his owner) notified all of her current and former students of the impending situation. Each person was invited to come to the barn and say goodbye to Rhino in his or her own way.

> One child used the opportunity to take some final photographs, while another braided the pony's mane and groomed him to perfection. Another little girl made a special mash for him nearly every night the week before he died. The mash included all sorts of treats that had previously been limited—Pop Tarts, candy canes and everything else that Rhino loved. He left the world happier—and fatter—than ever.

Conclusion

Even if a horse's death is expected, we are never be fully prepared for losing a loved one. We can, however, use this time to build a bridge between the past and future. While we cannot—and should not—control the grief that comes with losing a special equine friend, we owe it to our horses to ensure that their last moments are happy ones.   ∽

CHAPTER 8

Letting Go

s Dr. Jennifer King explained in Chapter 6, euthanasia is often the kindest decision a horse owner can make for a suffering horse. Nevertheless, it is not an easy one.

Even when it is clear that veterinary science can offer no hope for a suffering horse, we may hold onto the hope that the animal will miraculously recover. This is especially true when considering euthanasia outside of emergency cases. It is far easier to do nothing than to make a decision that will cause us pain, and that may conflict with our own sense that it is somehow wrong to admit that it is time to give up the fight.

Kimberly Maloomian, an "A" circuit hunter and equitation rider, was faced with this decision in 2003. Kimberly had recently lost her retired show horse, Polar Blues ("Blue"), to cancer when the health of her other retiree, Just For Kimberly ("Kim"), began to deteriorate. Kimberly recalls:

> *My grandmother had made the decision to euthanize Blue. This time the decision fell on my shoulders. What was I going to do? I had just lost Blue and I didn't want*

to lose Kim also. To this day, the memory of my giving permission to euthanize Kim and bury her next to Blue still creates a knot in my stomach—but I know in my heart it was the right decision. I knew, deep down, that it wasn't fair to let Kim suffer just because I didn't want to say goodbye.

The "Right" Time

Many owners struggle with the issue of timing when it comes to thinking about euthanasia. Some may ask themselves, "Is it time? Is this the right time?" Others may wonder if they are giving up too quickly because their beloved horse or pony has always rallied and improved in the past. Even the most skillful veterinarian or the most perceptive owner may find it difficult to know with any certainty when it is really "time."

Emergency cases are generally more clear-cut for most owners. The horse with the irreparably broken leg is a simple example of when it is easier or more logical to decide on euthanasia. For the owner of the aged horse or of the younger horse with a chronic condition, it is sometimes very difficult to objectively say, "It's time."

Robin Urciuoli, an amateur dressage and hunter rider, recalls the challenge in deciding to euthanize her elderly pony, Alice:

As her Cushing's disease led to progressively worse founder and colic, I had to wonder how many times she could fight back and win. It was torture for her, for me and for my family. No one wanted to give up as long as there was a chance that the next day she would be comfortable. I was so physically and emotionally stressed that I was sick for months, and my doctor threatened to put me in the hospital. Caring for Alice took every ounce of my being; the only way I could leave for work was by telling myself I would not be able to pay her vet bills if I lost my job. I was at work when I got the final X-ray results that showed that no option except euthanasia would ease her pain. I had not expected them to show anything different, yet I burst into tears.

I did not think I would not be able to look at Alice when I got home, but somehow I did. She was especially perky the next night, which made it even harder to go about making the necessary arrangements.

Many times, a horse that is seriously ill or injured may appear to be "normal" at certain moments. A horse with a serious lameness, for example, may still be beautiful, fat and shiny—making the final decision for euthanasia even more difficult. Kimberly Gatto recalls the situation involving a school pony who lived in the stall next door to her horse:

It was hard to accept the fact that Rhino was not going to recover, because he still looked healthy. When the medication kept his pain in check, he was perky as ever, pushing me into the corner as I cleaned his stall and nuzzling against my coat pocket for treats. He was the first to whinny and stomp the ground at feeding time. But when I picked up his foot and saw the coffin bone beginning to break through, I knew that his owner had made the right decision in having him euthanized.

Related Decisions

Deciding to euthanize a horse requires an owner to make many other decisions, which often come with their own challenges. For example, Chapter 10 outlines options for burial or other final resting places. Even the most detailed guide cannot make those difficult telephone calls any easier. It cannot make them go away either.

Throughout our lives, we are typically advised to plan ahead and are rewarded when we do. When it comes to euthanasia, the planning ahead part represents its own hurdle. Robin Urciuoli recalls:

I wanted it to be on a Sunday, so I could spend all weekend with her since I had no time off left at work. I arranged to page the vet when I thought we were ready. Over the last days, I doubted my decision, felt guilty about going to work, sleeping and every other necessary activity and was miserable around friends and family members who were trying to help. Cremation was out of the question because at that time it required "delivering the remains dismembered," and the pet cemetery was too expensive. We had land, so we decided to bury her at home. I thought there were certain people who deserved to be told in advance so they could take the opportunity to visit Alice one last time and say "thank you."

On the last morning she actually got loose and trotted outside to eat grass. I sensed it was her "last hoorah" and called the vet a few hours later. In the meantime, a family driving by our house stopped so the kids could pet her. I remember how hard it was to take her away from the grass toward the woods; she just wanted to eat. I remember it feeling sort of like an out-of-body experience, just doing what had to be done in a daze.

While some situations warrant that an owner struggle with a decision, other cases are more clear-cut. Some horse people feel that an animal will, in its own way, "tell" an owner when it is time to let go. Others believe that as owners, they will "know" when it is time. Owner/rider Ashlee Mansour experienced this with her horse, Parade, who had just recovered from a serious illness:

By the end of the second week she was starting to get back to her old self. I spent the weekend taking care of her. The next day, I received a call that she was down again. When I got there that night and looked at her, I knew it was much more serious than we'd thought. We pushed her onto the trailer and got her to the vet school as quickly as we could.

They took us into a room to view the X-rays and there, right under the shoulder, was a compound fracture. As the vet was telling me they could try to operate and insert a plate, I could see in his eyes that it would not be the best decision for my horse. She had other problems and they didn't know if she would make it through the surgery. All I could think of is that I couldn't put her through that kind of pain.

I went to see her one last time. She rested her head on my shoulder; she was tired. Then she licked my hand as I kissed her forehead. We both knew it was time.

Being Present–or Not

Once the decision is made and logistics are in order, we must determine whether or not to be present for the euthanasia process. Since this can be a difficult choice to make, it may be helpful to talk about the options. For example, a veterinarian can offer advice on what may or may not happen when a horse is euthanized. Learning more about the process from well-informed, objective people may help the owner answer his or her own questions, and may help dispel some of the "old groom's" tales that surround euthanasia.

After discussing it with her veterinarian, family and friends, Cindy Sydnor felt that the situation would be better for all involved if she said her goodbyes beforehand:

The day came. I did not go to the barn. I had already said goodbye to Lover many times and I felt that it would be too much to see him put down. I think that was a good decision. My friends and the vet were kind enough to take care of him for me.

Other owners feel compelled to be present as their horse passes on. And some animals, such as Kimberlee Quarles' pony, Misty, pass on quietly and peacefully.

Dr. Garfinkel returned to Misty to administer the merciful injection, which would end her suffering once and for all. Misty went down with grace and class, not wanting to further upset her little friend (my young daughter, Kiana). Dr. Garfinkel knelt down with tears on her cheeks, gently stroking Misty's head and face. She spoke to Misty in a comforting tone.

After what seemed an eternity, Dr. Garfinkel checked to see if Misty was gone. She slowly and gently removed Misty's halter and covered her body with a tarp. She walked to Kiana, who was sobbing, and handed her the halter. She hugged her and told her that Misty was at peace now. She explained to the young girl that she has a box for all the souls of the good horses she releases from pain. She explained that as Misty was leaving, she prayed for Misty's soul to go into her box of "Angel Horses." Misty was now an Angel Horse running free and feeling no pain. She told Kiana that Misty was happy and would watch over her forever.[2]

Not all horses pass so quietly, however. As Dr. King mentioned in Chapter 6, while a euthanized horse does not feel any pain, the animal may fall or appear to struggle as he or she passes on. This can be troubling to watch, particularly if one does not expect it. Robin Urciuoli recalls:

I can't remember if I thought about not being with her at the end; she had been through so much for me, I had to be there with her.

When the vet arrived, she administered a shot of tranquilizer, which made us have to literally push and pull to get her to walk the last few hundred feet toward the hole. The vet then asked if I was going to hold her. When I said yes, she warned me to be careful where I stood, as there would be no way to control how Alice went down. I remember thinking that my pony never hurt me before—she would not hurt me now.

I was on the other side of Alice's neck when the vet gave the first shot. She went down and began what appeared to be "extended trotting." I got up, screaming that I'd never forgive myself and turned to run away—then spun myself around, fell to my knees and whispered into her ear thanking her for being such a good girl. I told her that she could trot all she wanted now with my first dog at her heels, and I listed the people who loved her, while the vet physically struggled to get more shots into her. I knew it was finally over when I rubbed her nose and she "snuffed" my hand one last time, like she used to do when she looked for food but didn't find any.

Like any stressful event, once it is over, the feeling of relief may be profound. And, it may extend to others in the owner's and horse's circle. Understanding that the process will end and that this grief is shared by others may help an owner to decide if it feels right to be with his or her horse when he/she is euthanized. Lisa Carusone writes:

After it was all over, I remember hugging Sandy, Lucille's vet. She told me that she knew I'd feel better over time. She also told me that she thought I probably felt better already. And she was right.

My husband John was with me when we euthanized Lucille, and he'd stood by me like a rock during this time. But I also knew that I wasn't the only one in my circle who was up very early that morning. I had the distinct feeling that a number of other people were awake with me and were going through something similar to what I was experiencing. They weren't there with me physically, but were certainly there with me in spirit. Later on, when I was ready to talk about this, (my friends) Molly and Louise told me separately that they'd been awake, unable to sleep, in those early morning hours on the day Lucille died.

Guilt Feelings

The loss of a horse through euthanasia can leave us feeling guilty. Did we make the right decision? Was it too early or too late? Could we have done something differently? Your mind may be riddled with "what ifs" after your friend has passed on. This is part of the natural grieving process and will lessen with time.

Beware of others who may second-guess your decision or actions. Everyone has his or her own opinion and must make his or her own decisions. If you have thought it over and discussed all options with your veterinarian, you have made the decision that was right for you and for your animal. It does not matter what others think or feel about your decision. If others try to change your mind, respectfully change the subject or ask that they respect your wishes. Unless they have walked in your shoes, they are not in a position to make your decision for you.

Dressage rider Lendon Gray recalls the ending of her Olympic mount Seldom Seen's life:

Seldom Seen, or Brillo as we called him, was about 26. He'd lived a long and good life, and at the end, he had serious health problems. There was no doubt that it was time to put him down.

The decision was a fairly easy one for me to make, and I think it had something to do with my approach to death. Quality of life has meaning for me. When the time comes, I feel that we're doing them a favor by taking responsibility. For them, the real hardship began when they stopped being what they used to be. At the end, their hardship is over. For a horse dogged by age, illness or injury, death—I hope—is a relief, but we're the ones who seem to suffer more." [3]

Conclusion

Euthanasia can be considered an unselfish decision, in which we put our own feelings of sadness aside for the sake of our equine friends. While it is never easy to lose a great friend, euthanasia is often a part of responsible horse ownership.

PART III

The Final Farewell

I give you this one thought to keep—
I am with you still—I do not sleep.
I am a thousand winds that blow,
I am the diamond glints on snow,
I am the sunlight on ripened grain,
I am the gentle autumn rain.

When you awaken in the morning's hush,
I am the swift, uplifting rush
of quiet birds in circled flight.
I am the soft stars that shine at night.
Do not think of me as gone—
I am with you still—in each new dawn.

— Native American Prayer

CHAPTER 9

Falstaff

By Amanda Hogan
as told to Kimberly Gatto

osing horses is a part of life here at Windrush Farm. Many of the horses that are donated to our therapeutic riding program are getting on in years and are entrusted to our care for the remainder of their lives. In turn, their experience, training and wisdom prove invaluable to our many students.

Falstaff happened to have been quite young–10 years old, in fact—when he arrived at Windrush. A handsome buckskin with a vibrant blaze and a personality to match, Falstaff had been pony clubbed and evented successfully at the preliminary level before he began his "second career" with us.

Falstaff's kind disposition eased everyone into the horse world, no matter how tentative they may have been. He taught a frightened or handicapped child that it was safe to enter a horse's stall. He showed a youngster who was afraid to trust people that it was OK to confide in a horse. Falstaff communicated with folks who could not speak, and comforted those paralyzed by grief or pain.

I can vividly recall the day that a blind boy with autism came to the farm. Falstaff—who generally hid at the back of his stall—came right to the doorway and blew softly on the child's hands. He then stood patiently on cross-ties while the multi-handicapped child attempted to groom him. As we helped the child onto Falstaff's sturdy back, the horse actually moved his body towards the boy in an effort to help me hold the child up. Falstaff must have stood at the mounting ramp for 10 minutes while we made various adjustments.

Like most great teachers, Falstaff tailored his lessons to each particular student's abilities. A young girl who suffered from spastic diplegia (a condition that causes tightness in the muscle tone of the lower extremities) first learned to leg yield on Falstaff's back, teaching her confidence and poise. Watching the pair perform a demonstration ride was a truly heartwarming experience. Falstaff walked, trotted and cantered for her, totally independently, in front of hundreds of people—and never missed a step.

While disabled riders discovered comfort and strength in his gentle stance, able-bodied riders found Falstaff's mischievous personality a welcome challenge. Outside in the field, he would sometimes wait until his unsuspecting rider wasn't paying attention, and lunge to take a bite of grass, nearly pulling his rider over. Working in a line in a class, he was known to playfully nip the horse in front of him, all the while looking totally innocent. Then there was the day we found him totally bloated and burping apples after he had gorged himself under his favorite apple tree.

As partners in our program, Windrush horses build very important relationships with staff members, volunteers and students. Falstaff, in particular, had accomplished many "firsts" for our various riders: first events, first shows, first canters, first jumps, first beach rides, first trail rides. And in time, he would teach many youngsters another "first": how to let go.

Falstaff reached his 30th birthday in 2000 and began to show the telltale signs of age. Yet his graying hairs and angular back did not interfere with his continued lessons. His personality continued to shine, whether sneaking past a handler for a bite of grass or donning a festive Santa hat at the annual holiday party. And he became somewhat of a celebrity—Falstaff's work earned him Regional Therapy Horse of the Year honors in 2003 from the North American Riding for the Handicapped Association.

In early 2005, however, Falstaff began to have difficulty rising to his feet. Like many elderly horses, he would lie down to roll and simply be unable to get up. Oftentimes it would take three people to get him back onto his feet. We became worried that our beloved friend would become cast in his stall—or worse, become seriously injured while trying to rise—in the overnight hours, when nobody would be around to assist him.

After many discussions with our veterinarian, the difficult decision was made to humanely end Falstaff's suffering. Because he had been with us for such a long time and seemed so happy in his life, Falstaff's loss was exceptionally difficult for us. As you can imagine, we try to prepare all students and staff for the inevitable loss of our older horses. We monitor changes of behavior, condition and temperament and try to discuss them openly. The staff is quite candid with the volunteers, parents and students (where appropriate) because each person has a vested interest in the animals. The impending loss of a horse is always discussed with our students; they need to know that dying is a natural process and that euthanasia is a peaceful alternative for an animal that may be in pain or suffering.

We followed this protocol when we discussed Falstaff's impending euthanasia with our students and friends. All those who wanted to give special recognition or wanted to say goodbye to our dear friend were given the opportunity. We received numerous phone calls and notes from those who wanted to share their memories of a first ride or something they had seen Falstaff do in a class—something that made them smile. These notes, emails and messages were collected in a scrapbook that we now keep in the office.

On the day he was to be euthanized, Falstaff received the most unbelievable breakfast consisting of his favorite bran mash mixed with diced apples and carrots. A group of eight teenage girls showed up at Windrush early that morning to primp and pamper him. They placed flowers in his mane and tail and groomed his coat to a brilliant shine.

Everyone was given the opportunity to say their final goodbye to Falstaff before a staff member or two accompanied him to the field where he was to be euthanized. The vet gave Falstaff a small dose of tranquilizer before leaving the barn so that he would not feel any stress during this time. Falstaff was hand fed treats all the way to the field—even as the catheter was placed into his neck and the injection given. We were with him to the end.

After he was buried, all of the students and others who wanted to visit were allowed to bring flowers or mementos to Falstaff's grave—and continue to do so. His resting place is very visible and was chosen specifically for him. Falstaff can now look out over all of the farm's activities and, of course, his favorite apple tree. In his passing, Falstaff taught us one final lesson—that love can live on, long after we say goodbye.

There is an old Arab proverb that states, "The horse is God's gift to mankind." Falstaff was that special gift to all who were fortunate enough to know and love him.

CHAPTER 10

Burial, Cremation and Other Options

The ritualized burial of animals, which has been practiced in virtually every part of the world at some point in time, serves as a means of honoring animals that have endeared themselves to their human owners. Throughout history, horses have been buried in special locations chosen by their owners in a final tribute to the horse's life.

When Alexander the Great's Bucephalus succumbed to war injuries, the conqueror led a formal funeral procession to his grave, erected a large stone monument on the site and ordered nearby residents to celebrate the horse's memory in annual festivities. A city was subsequently named in his honor.

The great Man o' War was also given an elaborate burial. He was laid to rest beneath a larger-than-life bronze statue of himself at Kentucky Horse Park, surrounded by the graves of other champions. More than 2,000 mourners attended the funeral, which was broadcast via radio. As a unique honor, Man o' War's entire body was embalmed and placed in a giant casket lined with his racing colors.

Charles Howard, Seabiscuit's owner, preferred to keep his horse's burial private. Howard buried the famous horse in a secret location on his Ridgewood Ranch, planting an oak sapling at the site of the horse's final resting place.

While we would all like the "perfect" burial for our horses, our choices nowadays are often limited by financial or logistical factors. For most horse owners, the typical options are burial on a farm or in a pet cemetery, cremation, rendering or donation of the body to a veterinary hospital.

Farm Burial

For many, burying a horse at the owner's farm or one offered for this purpose represents a phase of the "circle of life" in which the animal is returned to Mother Earth. One may wish to bury a horse under a favorite tree, in a pasture or at the foot of a trail. Tannetta Dow, the owner of an elderly pony who passed away, recalls:

> *We lined (Molly's) grave with fresh evergreens, put a blanket over her, and covered her with evergreens, and then built a lovely stone wall around her grave. We renamed the field she is buried in "Molly's Field."* [4]

The act of burial in a special place can be comforting for an owner. There are, however, several factors that must be considered before burying a horse.

Many municipalities prohibit burying an animal on public or private property due to environmental and public health concerns. It is important to check with state and local authorities for a list of burial restrictions within that area. If burial is performed illegally, a town health department can require that the body be exhumed and removed from the premises.

Once permission for burial is granted, a backhoe is needed to dig the grave. The cost to hire a backhoe and operator varies by region and may cost up to several hundred dollars. If you do not have access to a backhoe, it is wise to keep the names and telephone numbers of local operators on hand. It is much more difficult to find information in a highly charged, emotional situation. Robin Urciuoli recalls her emotional state at the impending death of her pony:

> *For two days, the sight of the backhoe sitting next to the driveway made it difficult for me to get out of the car. My mom had thought out the logistics; the hole had sort of a ramp, there would be straw, a tarp, and more straw on top. Alice would have something soft to go down on, then be wrapped up and gently slid into the hole. I had never even thought about logistics—that the hole would need to be dug in advance, the backhoe would need to stay in the yard, or the backhoe operators would need two hours of daylight in order to bury my pony safely.*

The hole used for burying a horse must be deep (typically from six to 15 feet) and located specific distances from streams, water wells and buildings. This is to avoid harming other animals or plant life, or contaminating water sources with chemicals used in euthanasia drugs. A body not buried deep enough may easily be dug up by coyotes and other foraging animals. Unpleasant odors, flies/pests and airborne viruses are additional concerns with shallow burial.

In wintertime, particularly in the northern states, frozen ground may limit the ability to dig a hole for burial. If a horse's death is expected, owners may benefit from having a hole pre-dug on the property while the ground is still soft.

If burying a horse on private land, owners may wish to consider whether the land can be developed in the future. If so, bear in mind that is possible that the site of your horse's remains could be dug up or built over.

Burial at a Pet Cemetery

There are more than 150 pet cemeteries in the United States, many of which have specific sections devoted exclusively to equines. Some pet cemeteries offer more than one burial option, with costs ranging from a few hundred to many thousands of dollars. At Angel View Pet Cemetery and Crematory in Middleboro, Massachusetts, for example, a "country burial" (approximately $500) entails burying the horse in a part of the cemetery that is not open to visitors, with no headstone or burial marker. A "formal burial" ($1,000+) includes a headstone, burial of the horse in a section that is open to visitors and the option of viewing the body prior to burial. Some cemeteries will also arrange a memorial or graveside service.

Pet cemeteries sometimes offer horse owners the option of purchasing plants, benches or trees to be planted on the cemetery grounds in honor of their animals. Many cemeteries also offer a "remembrance wall" on which a horse's name, photo, birth and death dates and a tribute may be posted.

For an additional fee, pet cemeteries may offer a service for picking up the body and transporting it for burial. In cases of planned euthanasia, an owner may have the option of transporting the horse, while still alive, to the cemetery and having the horse euthanized by their own veterinarian at the burial site. Many pet cemeteries also offer cremation services, which will be discussed in the following section.

A complete listing of pet cemeteries in the United States is available at the International Association of Pet Cemeteries Web site at www.iaopc.com.

Cremation

Some pet cemeteries and veterinary hospitals offer the option of cremating a horse's body after death. The facilities used for this service are called crematoriums. During the process of cremation, the horse's carcass is incinerated until it reaches a state of ash. The remaining ash, which may weigh as much as 50 pounds, is odorless and may be stored

indefinitely. Cremation costs vary, but generally start in the $500 to $1,000 range.

At an owner's request, the horse's ashes may be returned to him or her for storage in a decorative urn, to be scattered in a favorite place for burial. Many horse owners request that the ashes be stored in a vessel so they may be taken along if the owner moves to another location. Most pet crematoriums offer a large selection of containers, such as biodegradable and non-biodegradable urns, wooden caskets and scatter boxes.

In the past, many owners opted against cremation, as an equine body was too large to fit into the crematory oven whole and, as such, had to be dismembered prior to cremation. However, many crematoriums now have the facilities to cremate an entire horse's body. Be sure to check with the cremation facility and specify if you would like the horse's body "fully" cremated. Some owners, particularly those of race horses, follow the old tradition of having the horse's heart, hooves and head (the "essence" of the horse) cremated, while the remainder of the body is buried or used in research. It is important to be specific about your wishes.

Rendering

Rendering is another option that is available for horse owners. Some owners feel that once a horse has passed, the spirit is no longer with the body. These owners may opt to send the body to a rendering plant. Others may choose rendering because no other options are available to them.

According to the National Renderer's Association, rendering is "essentially a cooking process that separates animal fats and proteins, thereby recycling them into usable products." In this process, a carcass is heated at a temperature between 250 and 300 degrees Fahrenheit (121 to 149 degrees Celsius), which kills any pathogens. The renderer then separates the remaining material into fats and oils that can be utilized in animal feed or in various industries. Some rendering facilities will provide a pick-up service for a dead animal, with typical costs ranging from $25 to more than $200.

Lisa Carusone opted to have her horse's remains removed by a local man who took them to a rendering plant in her region:

Calling Bud a "renderer" does him a kind of injustice. I think of him as an equine funeral director. He is a professional, guided by a personal code of ethics. He provides a necessary service to others at a time in their lives when they need not only his expertise, but also his compassion and sensitivity.

Burial for my beloved mare, Lucille, wasn't an option. So Sandy, Lucille's vet, gave me Bud's telephone number. They'd worked to-gether before, and she felt he was the best person to be part of the team. The date was February 24, 1998, and he told me that he'd be there. I called him the day before just to confirm. Over the course of his career, he'd probably had a million calls like mine, but you never would have known it from the sound of his voice.

Bud was already at the farm when we drove up at 6:45 that morn-ing. For all I knew, he'd probably been there for hours. That's how seriously he took his job that day. He parked his truck off the farm property, under some pine trees. When my husband and I drove up that morning, it looked just like an ordinary truck. And he looked just like an ordinary farmer.

He got out to shake our hands, and then told us that he'd just hang back where he was until Sandy arrived. We went on ahead, Sandy came along shortly after that, and after talking with her, Bud drove in behind her. Again, he put his truck as far out of sight as possible.

Once Lucille was gone, she didn't look like my horse anymore, which is kind of what I expected. She had died very, very peacefully, and while I knew she was at rest, I also knew that she wasn't in her body anymore. Somehow, she looked smaller. Her coat seemed to have changed color, from its bright chestnut to a dull red. The essence that made up the mighty Lucille was just gone. I stood up after I said my last goodbyes. I hugged Sandy and thanked her for her kindness. My husband took care of giving Sandy and Bud the checks I'd written out the day before. I shook Bud's hand again, and he said, "I'll wait until you're gone."

He knew what he had to do next. I knew what he had to do next, but he was as good as his word. I looked back one last time as we went down the driveway, and there was Bud, watching over Lucille, making sure that my last glimpse of her was a good one.

Donation to a Veterinary School or Research Hospital

If your horse dies at a veterinary hospital, the body may be buried or cremated at the hospital itself. Some hospitals also allow animal remains to be transported to their facilities for cremation or burial. (Please check with the equine hospital in your area to find out if this is an option.) Some owners make the decision to donate their horse's body for research purposes. Owners may feel comforted by the fact that their horse is ensuring that research is conducted for the sake of other horses. Veterinary schools or research hospitals regularly receive horses and ponies whose unique cases can support their ongoing research. However, if the idea of your horse's body being dismembered as part of the research process is distressing to you, burial or cremation may be a more suitable option.

Some hospitals may waive the cost of euthanasia if the body is to be donated for research purposes. You may investigate this option by contacting your veterinarian or the nearest equine hospital.

Conclusion

Making final arrangements for a horse's remains is a very personal decision. There is no right or wrong approach. It is important to follow your own feelings and choose the option that is best for your individual situation. The best advice is to be aware of what your options are well in advance, so that you do not need to make a rushed decision in a highly emotional state. Take the time to talk with your veterinarian and others close to you and your horse. They can provide you with important information, a variety of perspectives and give you the support you need to make fully informed choices.

You depend on your horse, but your horse also depends on you. When it's time, he will be counting on you for a good death just as you have given him a good life.

Regardless of whether you bury, cremate or donate your horse's body, the fond memories of your time together will be there to guide and comfort you through this difficult decision.   ᔆ

PART IV

Children and Loss

I know that it must be different,
now that I am no longer there.
I realize how much I was loved
and how much you did care.
I know it will be hard at first
when you look around for me.
Expecting to find me in my stall
or beside my favorite tree.
Someday you will begin to see
although it'll take some time,
the happy times you shared with me,
the memories are yours and mine.
I'll remember you, my friend,
and how much you meant to me.
So please don't grieve and don't be sad,
it was just my time to leave.

— Author Unknown

CHAPTER 11

Forget-Me-Not

By Jody Davidson

very little girl should have what she wants most in the world."

My father lay dying. The diagnosis of cancer had been unexpected and his decline rapid. From the time just after Thanksgiving, when the doctors had given him the bad news, until his death, we all had a mere 10 weeks to say our goodbyes.

My father and my daughter Lora Rachel ("LR") were kindred spirits, best friends. She called him "Papa Pia," a contraction of "Grandpapa" and the name of his grouchy Siamese cat. There was nothing he wouldn't do for her. Ice cream was a forbidden treat in our house, but my dad took it upon himself to treat her to her first Dove Bar. He marveled at her every accomplishment, no matter how small. It was my father who provided her with her first Breyer horse, in what soon became an extensive collection, so that she might better imagine the horse she'd someday own.

Of course, before long, the subject of a "real pony of her own" came up. My husband and I were not in a financial position at the time to consider even a lease situation. We were building a new business, and funds were tight. Though I desperately wanted to give my daughter the pony she longed for, I knew her path would probably have to follow my own—taking weekly lessons and catch rides whenever she could until we finally had the resources to underwrite a pony of her own.

One afternoon as I sat vigil in the hospital with my father, he looked at me and said seriously, "Every little girl should have what she wants most in the world. I know I won't be here for LR's next birthday but I want to be sure she gets the gift we know she wants. I want you to buy a pony for her ... from me."

It took me awhile, but I finally found the right pony. Though she was ice white, her name was Cinnamon which had been shortened to "Cinni" around the barn. We could never understand why someone would name a white pony Cinnamon, but when the weather warmed up and we were finally able to bathe Cinni, we discovered to our surprise that she was actually a paint who had grayed out. Like a giant version of the Magic Color My Little Pony, when Cinni was wet you could see the large sections of dark-skinned pigment where her spots had been. For shows, LR decided to call the pony "Forget-Me-Not," for she never wanted to forget Papa Pia and all that he had meant to her.

Over the next two years Cinni was the perfect partner for everything LR could dream up. When our family moved to Vermont, we were lucky enough to board Cinni with a great trainer, Joe Forest, at a facility ideal for pony adventures. The barn and indoor sat at the bottom of a mountain with miles of trails and untraveled logging roads that could be accessed from the farm's dirt road. LR would hop on Cinni in the morning, a lunch and snacks carefully stowed in her fanny pack and not be seen again until afternoon feeding.

This, of course was in the "pre-cell phone" days. We spent Thanksgiving day that year traveling to visit friends and returned on Friday. The light on our answering machine was solid red. The calls started at 7:00 a.m. Thanksgiving morning and stopped at 1:40 p.m. that afternoon.

"Hey Jody, it's Joe. Not to worry but Cinni looks a little colicky

this morning. Nothing major, just off. I've got one of the girls walking her and we'll see what happens. Have a happy Thanksgiving."

"Hi, it's Joe again. The walking doesn't seem to be helping so I sent for the vet. She's on her way. I'll let you know what happens ..."

"Joe again. The vet checked Cinni out and gave her something for the pain. She had to go on another call but she'll be back to see her in an hour or so."

"Jody, Joe. Cinni has started bleeding internally. The vet is on her way back. It doesn't look good ..."

"Hey ... The vet says she believes there's been a rupture, maybe the intestine. She recommends putting the mare down. Cinni's in a lot of pain. A decision needs to be made soon."

"Jody, I'm so terribly sorry, but we put Cinni down. I know you wouldn't have wanted her to suffer, and she was in a bad way. I was with her at the end, and she was calm. I've got a backhoe coming and we're going to bury her in the field at the top of the mountain. I'm so sorry ...."

I stared at the phone in disbelief. How could Cinni be gone? She was a young mare, just coming 12. She'd been a picture of near-perfect health. At Joe's request, the vet had performed a postmortem, where it was discovered that a tumor had grown around the intestine, strangling it until the pressure caused it to burst. Tumors are not uncommon in gray horses and ponies. There had been no warning signs except a very slight drop in weight, which had caused no real concern. In the past few weeks Cinni's work schedule had increased since LR had advanced to daily lessons.

LR had not heard the messages, and when I called my husband and her into the room to break the news, the sight of my tears unsettled her. I tried to explain as best I could, but when the story came out, she was inconsolable. Over the next few weeks she did not want to go to the barn—not to visit friends, not to take a lesson, not to help out with barn chores. She went from a child who had spent every free waking moment near horses to one who refused to even discuss them.

I didn't know how to help my daughter through her grief. We couldn't afford to buy another horse at that time; our savings wouldn't cover the cost of a replacement. Unfortunately, Cinni had not been insured, a mistake I've never repeated. LR couldn't be tempted to go out to the barn for lessons. Several times I approached her about perhaps visiting Cinni's grave so she could "say her goodbyes," but the answer was always a flat but determined, "No, thank you." It looked like it was going to be a very bleak Christmas.

As luck would have it, in mid-December I had to attend a nearby business conference. One of the vendors who had set up a booth was an Internet provider who was giving classes on what the Internet was and how to use it. Within minutes I had my first heady experience surfing the Internet and while the instructor tried to bring my focus back to the potential business applications of the Net, I soon realized the medium's full potential ... a national marketplace for ponies! I spent the day online looking at ponies for sale and lease and one in particular caught my eye. It was an ad placed by a pony breeder in upstate New York looking to offer a free lease on one of her broodmares to someone who would train and show it. I jotted down the phone number and called the number when I got home. The woman who answered was friendly. She had a number of ponies, some quite well known pony hunters. The mare in question was named Annie Mae. It was agreed a videotape would be sent, and we all—LR included—waited anxiously for it to arrive. It was the first interest LR had expressed in anything horse-related since losing Cinni.

Annie arrived in our barn just after New Year's festively attired in shocking pink leg wraps and pink pompoms braided into her mane. Though it was nearly midnight when she was finally unloaded, LR bubbled with enthusiasm. We settled the mare into a freshly bedded stall— Cinni's old stall. As we watched Annie dig into the fresh bran mash LR had made for her, my daughter asked me quietly if I "thought Cinni would mind?" I told her I thought Cinni would be happy that LR was sharing her love again.

LR and Annie's honeymoon period was not without problems. Green pony/less-advanced rider combinations often have to work out the kinks. And there was always the unspoken comparison ... Annie wasn't Cinni and never could be. But, in her own way, Annie was as sweet as Cinni had been. There were occasional fits of temper—on both sides!—but the partnership that they forged was a good one. Thanks to Annie, my daughter learned patience, tolerance and how to communicate what she wanted to a pony who might not understand the vocabulary. It wasn't long before LR was once again having the after-school drop her at the barn instead of our house.

One day in late spring, LR made an unusual request. She asked if she could skip her lesson. When Joe and I said that would be fine, she tacked up Annie and then stopped before mounting to pick a bunch of wildflowers growing along the side of the barn. As she walked the little pony out of the stable yard she called to me: "I'm going up to the top of the mountain. Annie and I are going to go see Cinni. To say thank you." As they trotted up the road, I finally knew things were going to be all right.

Over the years since then I've said "thank you" a lot: to my father for helping a little girl's dream come true; to Forget-Me-Not for making every one of those dreams a reality; to Annie Mae for teaching my daughter that the gifts we are given do not die with the giver but live on in our memories of them; and to all the other wonderful ponies and horses since then who have helped give my little girl what she wanted most in the world. ✍

CHAPTER 12

The Grieving Process for Children

By Doris Worcester, MSW, LICSW
and Kimberly Gatto

hildren have a natural and unique bond with horses. From these magnificent creatures, a youngster can learn to care for another living being and, in turn, will receive unconditional love. A trusted horse or pony can be a child's best friend and a source of pride or strength. Through daily care and horsemanship, children learn responsibility; through riding and competing, they develop confidence and self-esteem. A horse can provide a much-needed boost to a child with emotional or physical disabilities, or to a teen who is unsure of his or her place in the world.

Grasping the Concept of Death

The passing of a beloved horse or pony often marks a child's first experience with death. The loss of a horse—whether one's own, a school mount or a fellow boarder's—may cause a strong grief reaction. Children mourn in much the same way as adults do and can be supported through the process similarly. They can grieve as intensely and as long as adults. The difference between childhood and adult grief is often a result of the child's developmental stage and his or her cognitive grasp of death.

When her favorite school horse passed away, young DeeDee Hunter recalled:

> *On the way home I asked my mom if Irish would be OK. She told me that he was really sick but that the vet was doing all he could. When we got home, I went straight up to my room so I could be alone. I had never thought that anything bad could happen to Irish.*
>
> *The following day when I came home from school, my mom told me that Irish had died. Right then I ran up to my room and cried. It wasn't the type of crying you do when you get a cut; it was the type of crying that you do when someone you love has just died. I can still remember that I cried every night for two weeks.[5]*

Forms of Grief

Children can display a variety of reactions to the loss of a horse or pony. They may be intensely upset, act as if nothing happened or even act happy. These are all normal responses to their loss and may change over time. It is important to accept the child's personal manner of mourning, to validate her experience and help the child express her feelings. Provide the child with an age-appropriate explanation for the death, and be open to answering any questions that she may have. Be truthful and willing to express your own feelings in a suitable fashion. Let the child know that her thoughts, feelings and behaviors are normal, and that you will help her through the grieving process. Tell the child that although she may have very strong feelings now, and that they may ebb and flow, they will not last forever.

As Jody Davidson illustrated in her story, it is common for a child to want to withdraw for a while after losing a horse. She may suddenly avoid the barn or any talk of horses in general. This is the child's way of coping with the pain of loss. When she is ready, she will gradually regain her interest in horses.

Some children may have mixed feelings about the death of a horse. The child may have been uncertain about the relationship or may have been angry at the pony for different reasons. She may have been wishing for a new pony. Be alert to any "magical thinking" the child may have, where she believes her hostile thoughts may have caused the death of her companion. Challenge these thoughts and tell her they are normal but not causal; "just thoughts" can not possibly cause an illness or death. She may also be angry at her pony for leaving her, and this may be confusing to her. Let her know this is natural and help her express those feelings in appropriate ways.

If the child does not want to talk about the loss, respect her wishes, but try again over time. At those times, you may simply choose to talk about your own thoughts and feelings and ask the child questions without expecting any response. This teaches the child that it's OK to have feelings and share them. Kaylie Chaffee remembers:

> *I have never had so many bad feelings at once as I did that day. The worst feeling I had was emptiness—a feeling that still hasn't completely gone away. I cannot explain every emotion I felt or still do feel about Luka and that day, two and a half months later. What I can say is that Luka touched my life in a way that few 14 year-olds—or even adults—are lucky enough to experience. There will never be another Luka, and she will never be forgotten. This amazing horse, who gave so much to me, will always remain in my heart.*

Coping Strategies

Children often express and resolve their feelings through artwork, play, and behavior. Be sure to provide plenty of age-appropriate experiences. In whatever way you choose to help the child communicate her loss and feelings and express her emotions, she will more effectively resolve her grief. LR Davidson coped with her grief by writing a "book" about her experience to share with classmates. LR also found the support of her friends important:

> *I guess when something like that happens so suddenly you just have to cry it out. You cry and then you put your mind into something else. My friends at school were so supportive of me and if anyone made fun of me crying about Cinni, they would always stand up for me, which shows so much in true friends. One of my friends from the barn sent me a big stuffed toy that looked exactly like Cinni. To me, that proved her friendship.*

It can be helpful to encourage the child to keep mementos or meaningful items associated with her pony in a special place. Ask the child if she would like to create a memorial ceremony to say goodbye to her pony, and let her design the ritual. If the child's pony has been buried, ask if she would like to visit the burial site. Many children are helped by creating a living memorial of their horse or pony by planting a tree or garden in the horse's name. Children can derive great comfort from the simple act of visiting and caring for their memorial. DeeDee Hunter wrote:

> *Irish was buried behind the ring. I remember that someone made a special plaque with his name and a painted picture of him on it. It was never put outside by his grave, but stayed on the windowsill in the farmhouse so that it would not be ruined by the weather.*

Very young children may find it difficult to remember a horse or pony, and this can be distressing for them. Provide the child with pictures of the pony, particularly photos of the child and pony together. This will help the child not only remember the pony, but also their special connection to each other. Help the child recall the pony by talking about their connection to one another.

The New Horse

If you are planning on providing the child with a new horse, it can be helpful to wait a while before doing so. Creating time and space for the child to fully experience the loss of her companion will help her integrate and resolve the experience more completely, strengthening her coping strategies for future losses. Leaving the pony's stall empty may help in that process. Tell the child that you will wait for her to let you know when the time is right to get a new horse. If your financial situation warrants that you save up in order to purchase a new horse or if you must find an alternative situation—such as a free lease—it may be helpful to make the child aware of that.

Lingering Feelings

Remember that children are not born with a fear of death. They learn to be afraid through what they observe and experience in their families, peer groups and social settings. The death of a horse or pony can be an exceptional opportunity to teach a child that death is a natural and understandable process. LR Davidson wrote:

> *I will never forget the way I felt when I heard the news about Cinni. I hope my story will help you understand death and how to deal with it. It is like my Mom says, "Bashert" (a Yiddish word meaning "something that is fated to be"). That means, what is meant to be is meant to be, and nothing can truly change life's course.*

Conclusion

A secure and caring environment, where those around her truthfully talk about death and appropriately express their feelings can serve to strengthen a child's coping skills and help her develop a sense of mastery over a potentially overwhelming and confusing experience. The death of her horse or pony can then take on a greater and more universal meaning that will aid in future life transitions and losses.   ❧

PART V

When Horses Grieve

When we lose a horse,
that special place in our hearts feels so empty...
But we realize, as time passes,
that equines have a way of teaching us about loving,
about loyalty, joy and friendship...
And whatever we've shared in their presence
can never really be lost.

— Author Unknown

CHAPTER 13

Rhino

By Kimberly Gatto

hutney, my beautiful and feisty Thoroughbred mare, has never cared much for other horses. My theory has always been that Chutney—the true "diva" that she is—views herself as superior to every other creature in the world. Any horse coming within 10 feet of Chutney is met with pinned ears, clenched teeth, an angry squeal and, occasionally, a lift of the hind hoof.

When Rhino, a 30-something-year-old grade pony, moved into the stall next to Chutney, the poor gelding was destined for torment. I had no doubt that proud Chutney would immediately take a dislike to the scruffy buckskin. They were as different as night and day — she, descended from a long line of Kentucky champions, and he, a melting pot of many unknowns. And so the war began. Chutney would repeatedly nip at Rhino over the stall partition and squeal with disdain. The wall between them would quiver as she nailed it with her back hoof.

The horses' stalls opened to in-and-out paddocks, with a wooden fence separating the two. Poor Rhino could not get very far away from Chutney. You can imagine my surprise when, one day, I found Chutney stretching her neck over the fence, nuzzling the gelding's mane. Then, with lightning quickness, he turned around and bit her. In his harsh lifetime, Rhino had learned the art of self-defense and was not about to let a pretty mare boss him around.

From that moment began a friendship for the times. Chutney had met her match, and she loved him in her own way. During the day-time, the two would stand close, with only the wooden fence between them. Then came the morning when the barn manager found the two horses standing happily together. One—or both—had kicked down part of the fence and escaped into the other's paddock.

Chutney and Rhino spent the next several months as close pals. They stood together, head to tail, grooming each other and swishing away the summer flies. When one had enough of the other, they would go to their separate stalls. Occasionally, they would try to fit together in one stall. True to her character, however, Chutney always appeared to be a bit indifferent to her friend.

Rhino, spunky as he was, was prone to lameness. He had foundered in years past and, as such, had some soreness in his front feet. For a while, bute and special shoes appeared to keep him comfortable. When the lameness began to increase, however, a veterinary exam revealed that Rhino's coffin bone was beginning to erupt through the bottom of his foot. While his spirit remained strong, it soon became apparent that Rhino's physical condition was beginning to deteriorate.

With her friend confined to his stall, Chutney opted to stay with him. Every morning, she would walk outside into the paddock and meet Rhino at the back doorway to his stall. She often demanded that her lunchtime hay be placed right outside of Rhino's stall so that she could stand beside her friend.

With winter quickly approaching and no end to Rhino's pain, the pony's owner made the difficult decision end his suffering. When Rhino left on his final journey to be put down at a nearby farm, Chutney seemed to know what was happening. She bid her friend farewell with a strong whinny, and then, in true Chutney fashion, appeared to simply move on with her life. In fact, she promptly entered Rhino's empty stall

and gobbled up the breakfast that he'd left in his feed bucket.

It wasn't until a week later that I began to notice a change in Chutney. She would often stand in Rhino's doorway, just as she had when her friend was alive. Occasionally, she would enter his now vacant stall, her head hanging low. In many years of ownership, I had never seen Chutney acting like this. My feisty mare seemed sullen and dejected.

Having lost my father years earlier, I was all too familiar with the signs of grief. Just like a human, Chutney appeared to be grieving the loss of her friend. However, we humans could talk about the loss, cry on a friend's shoulder or even seek the help of a counselor. But how could I help my beloved horse grieve?

Rhino's owner, knowing how special the pony had been to Chutney and me, had given me a lock of thick black hair from the pony's tail. I decided to show the lock to Chutney. When I presented it to her, the mare took great delight in sniffing it. When I drew it away from her, she followed it. She clearly connected the scent with her friend. For a few weeks, I presented the lock to her to sniff on a daily basis.

Gradually, in her own time, Chutney became less interested in the lock of Rhino's hair. She also stood in Rhino's doorway less and less. Soon after, circumstances changed and we moved to a new farm. Eventually, another gelding won her affection.

When the time comes for Chutney to leave this earth, I will be devastated. I am hoping that I will find at least some comfort in the fact that she'll have a friend to greet her on the other side. She will approach him with pinned ears, clenched teeth, an angry squeal and a raised hoof. And together they will gallop over the beautiful Rainbow Bridge. ⁓

CHAPTER 14

Horses and Loss

Over the last 10 years, countless volumes have been written about equine behavior in an effort to help us better understand these animals that mean so much to us. Through such research, animal behaviorists have learned that horses, like humans, will often grieve for a lost companion. While it is unknown to what extent horses understand the process of death and dying, they and other animals are aware of the fact that a companion—human or animal—is no longer with them.

Horses by nature are herd animals—social creatures that follow a leader and conform to an established hierarchy or "pecking order." A typical herd includes a "boss" (or "alpha") mare and a herd stallion, along with subordinates; the weakest animals are at the bottom of the order. Horses instinctively want to remain part of the herd; an animal will typically only leave, or be driven from, a herd if he is ill or injured.

Like all herd animals, horses can form strong attachments to each other. Even horses that appear to have no interest in—or intense dislike for—one another when stabled or pastured together may pace or whinny frantically when separated.

Dressage rider Rachel Bigger describes her horses' reactions to the death of her blind Appaloosa, Tonto:

None of my other horses cared much for Tonto. They would chase and bite him, and he couldn't get away because he was blind.

The horses finally called for Tonto on that last night. They had never before; they'd never answer his whinnies. But when they all went into the barn and Tonto was still lying outside in the dark, they whinnied for him. I'm glad he heard that before he left us; I'm glad he finally heard them answer him. I guess they did love him after all.

Signs of Grieving

One of the initial signs of grieving in horses is whinnying or "calling" for the lost companion. Stabled horses may pace or stall walk, while those living outdoors may trot or gallop the fence line searching for the lost companion. Some horses, like Tommy in Chapter 3, may become excited when they see another horse that resembles their lost friend. Others may act depressed, with their heads hung low, showing little interest in their surroundings. They may pick at their feed or stop eating altogether. Some may crave extra attention from people, while others become more aloof. Similar to the human grieving process, each situation is unique.

A Sixth Sense

Some horses appear to have an innate knowledge when another equine is about to be euthanized or has passed on. There have been reports of horses "saying goodbye" to a companion by blowing into each other's nostrils. Other horsemen have reported animals acting strangely, displaying a "sixth sense" that a companion has passed on. Amy Neal remembers her horse Silver's reaction to the sudden death of his barn mate, Gerri:

> *Silver was noticeably upset that morning. His normally neat stall was "trashed," with hay and shavings strewn everywhere. When I put him in the round pen, he whinnied and paced frantically and could not be consoled.*
>
> *After Gerri was buried, I walked with Silver up to the gravesite. He walked slowly behind me, head held low. We stayed there for a little while. As I began to make my way back toward the barn, I turned to look back at Silver, who was still standing beside the grave. He looked up at me as if to say, "Give me a minute alone." After standing for a moment at Gerri's grave, he resumed walking back with me. It was clear to me that Silver was bidding his dear friend goodbye.*

Often, a horse will express interest in sniffing the body of a dead companion. Some animals will survey the body of a deceased companion in a pasture, for example, then continue grazing peacefully. A young foal who has lost its dam may find comfort from a blanket or other article of clothing that retains the scent of its mother. Tannetta Dow's foal, Hope, seemed to sense the death of Molly, an elderly pony to whom she'd become quite attached:

> *My vet suggested that once Molly had died, I bring Hope out to "see" her. My friend Theresa and I brought Hope down to Molly, who was now lying beside the grave, and let Hope smell Molly all over. She kept sniffing and in particular kept breathing into Molly's mouth. She would sniff Molly's whole body, but always come back to her mouth, and breathe into it. After about ten minutes of this she stepped away on her own accord and started grazing. She has not called for Molly since then.*

Herd Hierarchy

If the deceased horse was part of a herd, the remaining animals may need to work out a new hierarchy. There may be kicking and scuffles as the animals determine the new pecking order. Some herds may not react well to the introduction of a new horse soon after a loss. These animals may need to adjust to the loss before welcoming a new horse into the herd.

If a horse has lost its only companion (such as on a private farm of two horses), it may be beneficial to get a new companion immediately. Most horses are uncomfortable being alone. If the companion's death is planned in advance through euthanasia, it may be wise to bring a new horse onto the scene well in advance.

Like their human counterparts, horses will take time to move on from a loss. Owners must be patient to help a horse work through the grieving process. Horses are creatures of habit and thrive on routine. Therefore, moving a horse to a new stall or paddock after a loss may upset the animal further. Even subtle changes, like introducing a new feed or beginning to work with a new trainer may not be the best thing to do while the horse's grief is still fresh. As always, consult with your veterinarian with any questions regarding your horse's well-being.

Conclusion

Although it may seem unusual, it makes sense that horses would grieve the loss of another. As herd animals, they are bound together by instinctual behavior to find safety and comfort in numbers. When a member of the herd dies, instinct tells the surviving horses that something bad has happened, and they react accordingly. While we, as humans, may want to assign some of our own values to their grief, the sadness they may feel needs no additional explanation. ⊰

PART VI

Remembering a Special Horse

*Do not mourn my passing, for if you could only see
by slipping all my earthly bonds, I'm young again and free.
By day I run the heavenly fields, my body well and strong
At night I sleep at angels' feet, lulled by celestial song.
So do not mourn my passing, just close your eyes—you'll see
I'm once again that gallant horse, as you remember me.*

— Author Unknown

CHAPTER 15

Zip Always Belonged to God

By John Lyons

right Zip's never been my horse. He's been on loan to me from God for the last 28 years, and I will miss him. Zip developed a severe arthritis in his spine that affected his hindquarters. He got down and was unable to get up. That happened once or twice, and we were able to get him up again. God allowed us time to assess the situation, to love on him another six weeks, and to say our goodbyes. When he got down the last time, my wife, son and daughter-in-law were with me when the vet put him down for us. I thank God for all the years that I've had with him, and for what he's taught me about myself, and about God.

I've learned that God, like Zip, is forgiving. Horses don't bear grudges. No matter what you've done to them, when you stop doing the bad thing and get consistent in the good thing, they carry on as if the bad thing never happened. Zip never asked for a plush life. He just wanted to be my friend.

I've been in some rough situations and put Zip through hard times. For instance, on the ranch, when he was my only helper, he'd hold big steers and sometimes come home roughed up. It didn't matter. He was ready to go to work the next day.

And plenty of times I'd snub a mare up to him who was so mad she'd be ready to kick the tar out of him—and me. Zip would just maneuver so I could stay safe and help that mare in the process. He never chewed me out when we got back to the barn, or told me what a jerk I was for how I handled things.

Zip has been a constant in my life. Through many personal traumas and deaths in the family, Zip has always been there for me. And I learned a great lesson about life when Zip went blind after an anaphylactic reaction to a cold medicine. It was my decision to give him the injection, and he dropped to the floor immediately. I can't tell you how hard I struggled with guilt.

Though I'd taken all the right precautions, to think that I'd hurt Zip was a heavy weight. I took him to lots of specialists, and nothing could be done for his sight. But one vet told me something significant. He said that Zip wasn't upset by his loss of sight. He probably assumed that when horses turn 19, they go blind. Zip focused on life the way it is now, not what could have been.

It's a wonderful gift to have shared so much of my life with Zip. For now, go give your family and horses a hug and thank God for them, and for Zip, who has always been my perfect horse.   ❧

Reprinted with permission from **The Perfect Horse***, October 2003*

CHAPTER 16

Honoring a Horse's Memory

hen a person loses a special horse, whether through death, sale or other reasons, the loss can be devastating. Long after the loss, the memories of that animal live on in the person's heart. This chapter outlines tips and suggestions for paying tribute to a special horse. You may choose to use any or all of these, or incorporate some of them into your own unique tribute. You may also choose any of these options to help support a friend or family member who has lost a special horse.

Living Memorials and Markers

Many people choose to plant a tree or flower as a memorial to a special horse. As the plant or tree grows, it will serve as a reminder of the horse and all that he or she meant to you. Incorporate the language and legend of plants into your choice. For example, red roses mean love, yellow roses signify friendship and white roses represent peace. A little research into your favorite trees or flowers may help you find the right combination of beauty and message.

You might choose something that has special meaning to you or that is emblematic of your horse. For many Thoroughbred owners, the Kentucky Derby is a special event. The annual "Run for the Roses" might make a beautiful red rose the right choice to honor your own Thoroughbred, his or her heritage and place in your heart.

When you plant your memorial, you may wish to include other elements that will make the event uniquely yours. You may, as Jennifer Shirey did in Chapter 5, bury some of your horse's hair or another small, but special, keepsake in the soil. Adding a plaque or sign alongside what you planted in memory of your beloved horse is another way of creating a unique memorial.

For some, sharing a memorial feels like the right thing to do. Many pet cemeteries or veterinary hospitals will let you purchase or sponsor a tree to be planted in memory of your horse. Often, these trees can be marked to let visitors know that they're enjoying a thing of beauty that was given out of love and fond memory.

Benches put in a special place are another popular idea, and would be very welcome at your own home or in a more public setting. Whether rustic or more formal, benches offer a sense of permanence and the opportunity for visitors to sit, reflect and pay their respects.

If your horse has been buried, and if it is permitted, you may wish to purchase a headstone or plaque to mark the burial site. Many of the world's greatest—and the most humble—horses are buried with markers. From the Kentucky Horse Park to the famed Breakers Stables in Newport, Rhode Island, horses across generations have had their final resting places honored this way. You'll find several of these markers in pictures and on-line. You may find that historical reference points such as these will help you choose the stone or plaque that is right for your horse.

Kaylie Chaffee and her instructor took great pains to ensure that Luka's gravesite was unique and special. Kaylie remembers:

> *My instructor called me and asked if I was busy. She told me that we were going to go shopping for materials to build Luka's gravesite.*

I have to admit, I had been putting it off. I was afraid to go back to the farm because I hadn't been there since the day Luka died.

We walked into a couple of stores, having a few ideas in mind of what we wanted the grave to look like. We both agreed that we wanted a stone bench as her gravestone. We looked at all different kinds of flowers and bushes and trees. We decided to put the flowers in pots so we could rearrange them if we wanted to. We chose the colors burgundy, navy blue and white for the pots and flowers because those were our colors for our last show season together.

That very same day, we built the gravesite. We leveled out the area and laid white pea stone down over the entire grave. Then we put the stone bench and flowers in place. Luka's gravesite couldn't be in a better place. There are trees in the background that let just enough sun come through, and at the right time of day, the area almost looks heavenly. My mom said she noticed a change in me after we built the grave. I think it was because I felt Luka could finally rest in peace.

Memorial Services

Like many pet owners, you may choose to hold a memorial service that celebrates your horse's life. You may wish to invite friends over for a special dinner and to share memories of your beloved horse. You don't have to do something elaborate. A short and simple service at your barn or at the horse's gravesite may be all you, and those close to your horse, need to help feel better. The guest list should be uniquely your own, but as you look around, remember the people who were a less obvious, or perhaps, a more routine, part of your horse's life. It is easy to remember the veterinarians and farriers who saw your horse regularly, but think about others who knew your horse and who might like to be included in a memorial service to reach their own kind of closure.

Memorials can be something other than an event. Online tributes on pet loss Web sites such as www.petloss.com are an option. You might have the desire and the skills to build your own Web memorial where visitors can add their own tributes to your horse. The U.S. Equestrian Federation posted a separate e-mail address so friends and fans of Chris Kappler's Royal Kaliber could send their words of support and sympathy. It is another option to consider.

Many owners like to place a memorial notice in their local equine newspaper or magazine. Putting your tribute in a national publication like *Chronicle of the Horse* may feel like the right thing to do. The content you choose is up to you and the editors of the publication. Some tributes are very simple. Others share short stories or memories. All allow a public recognition of the horse's life and of his or her loss.

For Kimberly Maloomian, a magazine tribute served as a unique way of honoring the memories of Just For Kimberly and Polar Blues, who had been well-known show hunters. Kimberly recalls:

> *After my horses passed on, I put together a memorial for the* Horsemen's Yankee Pedlar *magazine. This memorial featured a beautiful photograph of the three of us at a horse show years ago. Under the photograph, I wrote:*
>
> *"IN HONOR OF THE TWO HORSES WHO DEFINED MY JUNIOR CAREER"*
> *Only a few people are so lucky to say they have had the horse of a lifetime; I am blessed to be able to say I have had two. I will never have another with as much heart and forgiveness as you both did, thank you for teaching me how to ride, how to win and lose, and most importantly how to be a horseman. I could never repay you for all you have given me—neither of you will ever leave my heart."*

Some horse owners may want to share their thoughts with friends, but in a less public setting. Sending cards, announcements or emails letting others know about the loss of a horse is another approach.

Awards

If your horse was a show ring competitor, you may wish to establish an award as a unique way of honoring his or her accomplishments. You could sponsor a scholarship for a young or disabled rider. A school horse may be memorialized with an award for a riding student or camp rider in need of financial assistance. The choice is yours, and show managers and organizers can give you more guidance so you find the right tribute for your special friend.

Keepsakes

Keepsakes serve to preserve memories of a special horse or pony. There are as many options as there are horses, so let your creativity be your guide.

You may wish to create a plaque for the horse's barn area or stall, or a collage of photographs of your days together. You can make a wreath of photographs and ribbons from the horse's career. There are some unique ideas available for making throws or pillows out of your show ribbons. You may assemble a memory box to hold keepsakes such as mane and tail hair, a special halter, bridle or cooler.

You may also wish to create a scrapbook. Have your friends each write something about the horse and what endeared him or her to them. Some folks choose to frame photographs and hang them in the tack room. You may wish to make a photo frame from your horse's shoes, decorated in your stable colors.

Bracelets made from a horse's tail hair are gaining in popularity and are an extension of Victorian-era mourning jewelry. A century ago, when mourning rites for people were more elaborate and a larger part of social custom, the bereaved would often have hair from their lost loved ones woven into jewelry. There are a number of individuals and companies that produce this kind of keepsake; many can be located online.

You may choose to print out a copy of a special poem, such as The "Rainbow Bridge for Horses", and frame it along with a photo of your horse. Hang it in a special place that will bring you comfort.

Helping Others

Often, owners find comfort in making a donation in the horse's name to a veterinary hospital, a horse rescue organization or a riding program for the disabled. If the horse died of colic, for example, you may wish to donate to a colic research fund to help find a cure for the condition. Your veterinarian may be able to help you find just the right organization.

You may use your time to volunteer to a horse charity or rescue organization. Form a support group, even if it's informal, with others who have lost horses. Sharing stories and helpful tips with others, even over a cup of coffee, may do wonders for you as you work through your loss. Support a cause, such as rescuing off-the-track racehorses or elderly equines that are abused or neglected. Volunteer at a therapeutic riding program. Helping a cause may provide comfort during the grieving process, and it is another way to honor your horse.

Perhaps you'd like to tell your horse's story in a book or magazine in order to raise awareness of a disease or illness that claimed his life, or simply to serve as a memorial. While the popular equine publications cannot print everything they receive, contact them to see if your story or article might be just what they're looking for. If you built a Web site to honor your horse, consider adding to its content with your story.

Organize a trail ride or horse show in your horse's name, and donate the proceeds to a worthy equine cause.

You can be as busy as you want to be when you help others. Consider your resources—personal, professional and financial—as you volunteer your time. Remembering your horse in this way does not have to become a job unto itself. Do what feels right and know that your efforts will be appreciated no matter how small or how big.

Cultural Memorials

Many cultures have unique ways of honoring lost loved ones. You may wish to take part in some of these traditions. Look to your own ethnic heritage for ideas.

For example, are there rituals you're already familiar with or already practice that might be adapted in a way that respects the tradition but allows you to use it differently? Perhaps its as simple as saying a special prayer for your horse. Perhaps it's more elaborate, but if it's already a part of who you are, consider using it for this purpose.

You may find options in other cultures that are not your own. As discussed earlier, many cultures have specific ways in which they honor horses. The Lakota dance stick described in an Chapter 2 is a ritual you can adopt and adapt in a way that suits you. While it may feel strange to pick and choose your rituals, you are honoring your unique relationship with your horse and the unique characteristics of your loss. If it feels right, and if it is respectful to your horse and to the culture you are borrowing from, go ahead and do it.

Conclusion

Horses, famous and not so famous, live on in the hearts of their fans, owners and riders in part through the kinds of memorials and rituals described in this chapter. Commemorating a special horse in a meaningful way can be extravagant or more subdued. The important consideration is that the approach meets the unique needs of those who were intimately connected to the horse.

PART VII

Other Types of Loss

We who choose to
surround ourselves with
lives even more temporary than our own
live within a fragile circle,
easily and often breached.

Unable to accept its awful gaps, we
still would live no other way.

We cherish memory
as the only certain immortality,
never fully understanding the necessary plan.

— *Irving Townsend, from Separate Lifetimes,© 1986*

CHAPTER 17

Loss Other Than Death

hile the majority of this book has focused on the death of a horse, there are other kinds of loss that may be as difficult to overcome. Equestrians may grieve the loss of a horse through sale, theft or the end of a lease.

Horses change hands all the time and for any number of reasons. Children outgrow their ponies, and parents may have to sell one pony if they want their child to have another. Beginner riders who advance may find that their perfect first horse is not the right horse to help them move up. And sometimes we find that the horse we thought would be perfect for us, really isn't.

Life can have a funny way of interfering with our riding plans. For the college-bound teenager, it may be time to sell the horse. Family responsibilities may keep mom from getting to the barn for weeks on end. Divorce may mean that the horse has to find a new home, too. A change in fortune, such as a job loss or other family crisis, may force the sale of a horse. Whatever the reason, and no matter how many good things may ultimately come out of the sale of a horse, the process may still be a difficult one.

Perhaps the sale of a horse you love is completely out of your control. The horse may be owned by someone else who has decided to sell him. Or you may have grown attached to a camp or lesson horse that isn't there when you come back the next summer. While it is not possible to discuss every possible situation within the constraints of this chapter, we have highlighted some of the most common scenarios.

Outgrowing Your Horse

One of the most common reasons for selling a horse, particularly when it comes to children, is outgrowing the animal. The child may be simply too big for the pony or is ready to move beyond the abilities of the horse. This can be particularly upsetting. Kimberly Gatto remembers her sadness at the realization that she had outgrown her Connemara pony, Irish Spring:

> After my lesson, my trainer took me aside and told me it was time to move onto a horse. I lowered my eyes, pretending not to hear. I knew that one horse was all we could afford, so I'd have to sell Irish Spring in order to get a larger animal. I hoped that my trainer would forget the conversation or change his mind, but he mentioned it again to my mom the following day.

> I went home and cried, as did my mom. I knew deep down that Irish Spring needed a younger, beginning rider, like I'd been three years earlier. But I just could not imagine letting him go.

> In the end, it was comforting to hear that a little girl's family was buying Irish Spring. She was younger than I'd been when we bought him, so I hoped he'd have many more years with her. I never met her, which may have been better. I imagined her as a sweet, caring little girl who loved my pony as much as I did.

Feeling sad or upset about selling a trusted horse or pony once the rider has outgrown it may extend to the parents, trainers and others who knew and worked with the pair. While adults typically try to ease their child's concerns by not showing their own, they may also be touched by the transition.

The author's mother, Ann Gatto Urquhart, recalls:

> *I cried many times after we sold our pony, but I kept my feelings to myself because I didn't want to upset my daughter. For years afterward I thought about Irish Spring … where was he? Was he happy? I thought about trying to track him down but convinced myself he'd be impossible to locate. Maybe deep down I didn't want to know in case he was unhappy or had died.*

Time Constraints

For some horse owners, the time constraints of work and family life make it difficult to give a horse the attention it needs. Amy Neal was faced with selling a beloved young horse because of the challenges of managing a farm, teaching and raising a family:

> *I had acquired Zip, a young, once-in-a-lifetime horse. He was everything I was looking for in a partner. Although I was not yet ready to replace my current horse, I could not pass up the opportunity to begin training this youngster.*
>
> *After a year, I realized I just did not have the time for two horses. I could not justify the money required to support them both when Zip was fast becoming a "pasture ornament." He deserved more.*
>
> *After careful consideration, I made the very difficult decision to offer Zip for sale. I made a list of what was most important to me in his*

*new home. First on my list was that his new home would be loving
and permanent. Second would be whether on not the new owner
could bring him to his true potential. Selling price and personal feelings for the prospective buyer came in near the bottom.*

*I then took a long hard look at those who were interested in Zip to
see who best fit my top priority. I decided to compromise my personal
feelings and finances and chose a person whom I felt would love and
care for him for the rest of his life. Although I will always question
my decision to let him go, I do feel I made a good choice.*

Suitability

A famous event rider and trainer, in an unguarded moment, said
that the toughest horse/rider combinations for him to train were those
in which the horse and the rider were ill-matched to each other. He said
that the most challenging of those pairings was the overmounted rider,
where the horse was "too much'" for the rider to work with successfully
and safely. Not only was it hard for him to help them progress, but he
felt, at times, that the rider was in some danger.

He said that he'd tried any number of approaches to help his
students understand and act on his concerns. He'd been direct, he'd been
cajoling and he'd tried being a friend. In the end, the riders agreed with
his assessment. When he raised the issue of selling the horse, they all said,
"But I love him!" "And, he said, he was certain that they did."

Sometimes, he acknowledged, we fall in love with a horse that is
just not "right" for us. It happens for many reasons. We may be taken
with the way the horse looks. It may remind us of a horse we lost or
of a favorite horse from our past. The horse might have a terrific com-
petition record and, on paper, have what it takes to be able to take us
where we want to go. Perhaps the seller has been persuasive, or we may
have been looking for some time and been disappointed when things
haven't worked out with other horses, so we convince ourselves that
we've found the "right" horse.

For anyone who has gone through the process of buying a horse, it can be painful to realize that a new horse really is not "right." Beyond the time and expense of looking for the horse, we're left with an animal that we probably don't want to or cannot ride, yet we have to sell it before we can buy a horse that will be a better match.

We also may be left with a sense of personal shortcoming or failure. Like other athletes, riders have egos. To find out that your new horse is beyond your skill level may be more than just disappointing.

Trainer Jill Swift experienced this scenario with her horse, Ypres:

After two years and many setbacks, I came to the painful conclusion that Ypres was not the right horse for me. As a riding instructor/ trainer whose job it is to teach people how to ride their horses (and how to get through the tough times with them), it was difficult for me to admit to myself that this relationship with Ypres was not going to work out for either of us. It seemed to me that continuing would not have been fair to myself or to him. One week after my "epiphany," Ypres had a tantrum and bucked me off. I ended up in the hospital for emergency surgery, with a crushed wrist and dislocated elbow. I guess I was a little late in acting on my epiphany.

Choosing to sell a horse that is not right for you may leave you with more than just a bruised ego. You've realized that this horse is not the best partner for you. You still have the horse and need to find him another home. And yet, you've come to love the horse and feel a sense of responsibility to him.

It may help to consider the issue from the horse's perspective. If the horse is not right for you, you may not be right for the horse either. The bold horse with the timid rider may be just as confused and upset as the rider on his back. The older dressage horse with the up-and-coming young rider may find it difficult for his aging body to meet her demands.

Selling the horse that is not right for you is a loss in itself. However, it may be a kind of loss with a silver lining—for both of you. Jill Swift recalls:

We showed Ypres unsuccessfully to a handful of people and then, much to my dismay, a petite, blonde 14-year-old girl—who looked like she should have been looking at ponies—came to see him.

To my surprise, the girl loved Ypres instantly and he didn't seem to mind her affection. It was like she was searching for her new best friend in a horse-suit, and found him. My friend Katie and I held our breath as we watched this girl 'ride' Ypres. It was amazing! Ypres loved her because she didn't ask for or demand even close to what he was used to having to give Katie and me; he was basically off the hook of having to do any hard work for a while. After dismounting, she dangled from Ypres' head, hugging and kissing him (which he seemed to enjoy) and it was a done deal.

At that moment I swallowed a truckload of pride and realized that Ypres had found his person, and there is in fact a horse out there for each and every one of us.

End of a Lease or Contract

The ending of a lease can be upsetting for a rider who has grown to love the animal. As the owner of a horse, what could be better than to find a lessee who is as concerned about your horse as you are? And for a lessee, there may be a terrific benefit to having a relationship with a horse without the constraints of ownership.

Some leases may go on for years, open ended, with owner and lessee happy to continue. Others may be for a more defined period of time, with specific terms and conditions. While some lessees are casual riders, others show these horses and, leased or not, are looking for a level of performance and capability.

Many famous pairings are situations where owners contract with a rider to take that horse to the upper levels. Those riders become associated with those horses to the point where fans think the rider actually owns the horse. Think of Michelle Gibson and the late Peron, or Lisa Wilcox and Relevant. Regardless of discipline, these contractual arrangements may change, and pairings may come and go.

What makes successful lease pairings is the same thing that makes successful pairings where the rider owns the horse. Rider and horse are well suited to each other and to the level at which they are riding. Rider and horse have a good relationship and work well together. And, finally, rider and horse have a bond.

Breaking that bond, even if the rider knows the relationship may be only temporary, is still a form of loss.

Sale of a Horse That You Do Not Own

Anyone in the business of breeding, training or selling horses will certainly confront this challenge at some point in his or her career. While it may be the nature of the business, it would be erroneous to say that horsemen and women don't have special places in their hearts for some of the horses that have passed through their hands. Some may see their former charges doing well in the show ring, or may even maintain a relationship with the new owner. Many may wonder what ultimately happens to those horses.

Mandy Hogan recalls her feelings when Chutney, the horse she'd trained from a yearling, was sold at age 8:

> *One of the greatest fears I deal with on a regular basis is what happens to the horses I work with and care about after they move on.*
>
> *Many years ago I helped raise and train a lovely bay Thoroughbred filly named Chutney. She was easy to "back" as a 2 year-old, but in her third year she became a bit of a "hellion." She grew into a tough, opinionated little horse—too much for our therapeutic riding program. On the other hand, she was a talented, honest, sensitive horse who would give 110 percent if she liked you.*

When it came time to sell Chutney, I competed her to give her visibility. We developed an even stronger relationship, and I was absolutely heartbroken that I was unable to buy her for myself. I was mostly concerned that because of her particular temperament that she might easily be misunderstood and abused. Certainly these fears were confirmed by some of the individuals and trainers who came to look at her. They always knew better than me what Chutney needed. I dreaded the day that someone would buy her and then sometime down the road, I would find out that she had been abused and/or had broken down.

Chutney was sold, and I lost touch for some time. I continued to wonder and then a note appeared in the mail. Imagine my delight in finding out that Chutney had found a life-long home with a young woman who still has her now, 20 years later. She had understood Chutney's sensitivities and idiosyncrasies and gave her the most wonderful life. What a relief to find someone else in the world who valued her as much, if not more, than I did.

Web site bulletin boards are full of people "looking for Smoky, a horse that belonged to a friend" or asking if anyone has "seen Ripley, a horse I rode at summer camp." Perhaps the person asking the question will get lucky and find that Smoky is a pampered pet in a neighboring town. Others may never know where their old friends have gone. Sometimes the "not knowing" is worse than having an epilogue, no matter how tragic, to the story.

Gaining closure under these circumstances can be difficult. However, as in the case with an old friend who drifts away, you may find comfort in focusing on the memories of the time shared together and kindnesses exchanged.

Theft

One minute your horse is there, the next minute, he's gone.

Horse theft has been an issue for centuries, and in the past, punishment for this crime was severe. Without a horse, it was difficult to travel or to farm. Horses were a necessity and had value to their owners perhaps beyond what they have today. Until Henry Ford invented the automobile, the theft of a horse had implications beyond the loss of a friend.

In the past, branding was one way to help an owner recover a horse. Today, we still have it in the form of hot or freeze branding. We can microchip our horses to recover them if they are stolen.

But what do we do if all our precautions still don't prevent someone from taking one of our horses? Debi Metcalfe, founder of Stolen Horse International, located online at NetPosse.com, wrote:

> When a horse is missing, someone needs your help. When our horse, Idaho, was stolen in September 1997 from our pasture in North Carolina, I turned to the Internet for help. I was unable to find any specific resources online to help us in our search, so I started gathering e-mail addresses from Web sites so I could contact them about Idaho. Unknowingly this work started building a network of people willing to assist in the search for stolen horses; that network is now called Stolen Horse International. We recovered Idaho in September 1998 in Tennessee after her flyer was seen on a convenience store's door, and we received an anonymous call that helped us find her.[6]

The Internet makes it far easier to let others know that a horse is missing and what it looks like. It allows you to connect with people who can help in your search and offer you their support and kind words. Unfortunately, sometimes even the most dogged of searches ends in failure or, perhaps worse, never ends.

Losing a horse to theft will bring up the kind of emotions felt with other kinds of loss. Feeling guilty or somehow responsible for the theft is common. Wondering if you did as much as you could to recover the horse may play on your mind.

Retirement

The retirement of a horse may also be viewed as a type of loss, particularly when the horse moves on to another home. Many high-level competitive horses, for example, are retired to a life on lush pastures, which may involve a change in ownership or geographical location.

For some, such as Olympic gold medalist Melanie Smith Taylor, the story can have a happy ending. Melanie was fortunate to be reunited with Calypso, the horse she rode to a number of key wins, including the 1984 Olympic team gold medal in show jumping, in his retirement. Nancy Jaffer wrote on equisearch.com:

> *Melanie retired from show jumping in 1987 and at the end of Calypso's career, he was sent for sale to Rodney Jenkins. Financial problems at the farm for which Melanie used to ride meant she was barred from buying Calypso. It seemed the two of them would never get together again.*

> *Then her husband-to-be, Lee Taylor, stepped in. He got in touch with Jenkins, never mentioning Melanie, and struck a deal. Calypso soon had a new home at Taylor's farm in Germantown, TN, where he was reunited with Melanie.*

> *"I was so excited to see him," she remembered. "I rode him around the farm the next day. There was a 4-foot wooden fence around the track, and I headed toward it and jumped into the ring and out the other side. I took off galloping, because I felt like a kid again."*

> *That was the last time Calypso wore a saddle. Retirement agreed with him. He looked "like a Thelwell pony enlarged. No girth would ever fit him," Melanie said.*

> *"For 14 years, he admired the young fillies in his pasture, wallowed in the lake, snoozed in the sun and munched grass to his heart's content. The morning before he died (in December 2002, at age 29), he galloped across the field as usual towards his beloved feed tub."*

> *[That] fall, Syd Eustace Goodrich, Calypso's loving caretaker during his career, came down to see him for what turned out to be a*

*final visit. Melanie was glad the three of them had a chance to be
together again.*[7]

Conclusion

When a horse moves on, one of the most common feelings associated with that transition is guilt. You may feel that nobody could care
for the horse as you did and, therefore, you are doing him a disservice
by selling him. Even though he may not be right for you and you both
would be better off by finding him a new home, you may still feel some
pangs of regret. If your relationship with the horse has been a good one,
but some other factor forces a sale or makes it the logical thing to do, you
may feel real conflict and turmoil over your decision. Losing a horse to
theft may bring up related feelings of guilt.

While we can never guarantee a wonderful life for our horses
after we sell them, we can take precautions throughout the sales process.
We can interview and screen prospective buyers, checking their refer-
ences and trying to the best of our abilities to ensure there is a good fit
between them and the horse. While it is not typical, it is possible to offer
to take the horse back if things don't work out. There are any number
of insurance policy-type actions you can take to try and make the best
match between your horse and a new owner.

In the end, and in the case of all of these scenarios, it comes down
to doing your best and then letting go. ⚘

Part VIII

Beyond the Rainbow Bridge

Don't cry for the horses that life has set free,
A million white horses forever to be.
Don't cry for the horses now in God's hand,
As they dance and they prance in a heavenly band.
They were ours as a gift, but never to keep,
As they close their eyes forever to sleep.
Their spirits unbound. On silver wings they fly,
A million white horses against the blue sky.
Look up into heaven, you'll see them above -
The horses we lost, the horses we loved.
Manes and tails flowing, they gallop through time,
They were never yours, they were never mine.
Don't cry for the horses, they'll be back someday,
When our time is gone, they will show us the way.
Do you hear that soft nicker? Close to your ear?
Don't cry for the horses,
love the ones that are here.

— © Brenda Riley Seymore

CHAPTER 18

Loving Another Horse

By Lisa Keer Carusone

I told my husband that I was ready for a Telaraña bracelet this Christmas. I already have a Lucille bracelet. You've seen them, those bracelets you can buy and have engraved with your horse's name. You get your choice of a brass or silver plate on a black or brown leather band, snap or buckle closure. I think every young girl or woman who rides has at least one of them, and I'm no exception.

To me, these bracelets acknowledge the unique connection between horse and human that goes beyond the idea of ownership. I always cringe a bit when I hear myself referred to as my horse's owner. There is something about that word that ignores the unique partnership we have. A partnership means that both parties complement each other and bring their unique strengths to bear in a relationship that strives for balance. Sometimes, one partner carries and supports the other. The balance shifts, and the weight is redistributed. And on it goes, a constant give and take.

Now, I am not naive enough to think that riding is a particularly democratic sport on any level. But if Lucille was going to have my name on her stall door as her partner, I wanted her name on my wrist.

Lucille left me on February 24, 1999. Telaraña arrived on April 1, 2003. It took me four years to find her, and it's taken almost two more for me to be ready to wrap her name around my wrist.

It's not like she's ever done anything to deserve taking second place to the memory of a dead horse she never knew. On the contrary, Larana, as she's called, is probably the most extraordinary horse I've ever known. Bred and started by Paul Belasik, she came to me as an almost 4 year-old, having already demonstrated the potential to be the upper-level dressage horse I'd always wanted. As anyone who sees her will tell you, she's just gorgeous. And brave. And unflappable. And … well, you get the idea.

After I had Lucille put down, I really didn't want another horse. I had Eire to ride. An Irish Sporthorse, Eire belongs to a friend of mine, and for me, it was the perfect situation. Eire was, and still is, a great horse. I could ride almost whenever I wanted and, better yet, she belonged to someone else. Someone else had to worry about her. Someone else had to make all the tough decisions. While I cared about Eire, and still do, I selfishly enjoyed being just her exercise rider.

Over time, I thought I might be ready for a horse of my own again. Eire was getting older, and I was ready to get more serious about my riding. Friends of mine had been after me for years to get a horse. "Just get a horse. What's the big deal?" they would say. But I did not want just any horse. It had to be between the ages of … already doing … no bigger than … a mare, and the list went on. Needless to say, my search had gone on for a while.

Larana fit almost every one of my requirements, and buying her was one of the most dispassionate decisions I have ever made in my life.

Someone once told me she had "everything in the right place." That was true. She had great parents. She had been started by one of the best dressage trainers out there. Her pre-purchase exam results were flawless, her behavior impeccable and she was so pretty.

Before she had even arrived, I already had a stall plate, halter plates and blanket tags made up with her name on them. But no brace-

let. I still wore Lucille's every now and then. I always had it on when I went into the show ring on Eire, and then, on Larana. I used to tug on it before I went in. I don't know if I was yanking myself back into the past or forward into the future.

In some sense, Larana made it tough for me to love her and to become her partner. She was young and talented. She wasn't chronically ill. She wasn't in pain. She didn't need me to worry about her the way I'd worried about Lucille toward the end of her life. The demands she made on me were very few. She needed me to keep her happy and healthy. With what she brought to the table, even I could do that.

I was not quite ready for that.

After two years of trying to repair a horse that could not be repaired, I made the decision to have Lucille euthanized. I chose to end my partnership with her. A good end was the very least I could give her. I didn't regret taking the long road to get there, even though she carried most of the weight of our partnership during that time.

Years ago I was told that horses and other animals have no sense of time or of the passage of time. I don't think that's true. To me, Larana always seemed to be biding her time, waiting patiently until I was ready to come around and be her partner. Waiting until I was ready to take more than just responsibility for her. Partnerships, as I said before, are all about balance, and like Lucille before her, she has probably carried most of the weight of our partnership during our time together.

Lucille's bracelet was brown leather, brass plate and buckle closure. Larana's will be black leather with a silver plate and a snap closure. Sure, it will look different than Lucille's, but what's important is that it will work the same way. It will represent the long road to the beginning of a new partnership. It will be different, not the same as what I had before, but equally valuable in its own right. ⌐

CHAPTER 19

A New Beginning

After losing a horse, people have varying ideas as to when they will allow another horse into their lives. For some, the thought of not having a horse to love is unbearable, and they begin looking for their next horse right away. Others need time to heal before opening their hearts to another equine. It may take them time before they are ready to consider another horse, and then it may take even more time before they find the right one. Regardless, most will eventually find themselves with another horse.

Mixed Feelings

Welcoming a new horse into one's life is typically thought of as a happy event. However, when the new horse is replacing one that has died, it may trigger mixed emotions. You may feel as if you are not being "loyal" to the memory of your lost horse or that you are somehow betraying your old horse when you begin to bond with another or even when you begin looking for a new horse. You may worry that it seems as if you are trying to "replace" the horse you have lost. You may ask yourself, "Has it been long enough?" or "Would my beloved horse approve of this new mount?" Perhaps you wonder if you even deserve this new horse.

The nature and circumstances of your loss may influence how you feel. While a loss of any kind is a painful experience, you may experience different emotions and a longer or shorter recovery time based on the specific circumstances of your own loss. Your attitude toward death and loss may also have some bearing on how you move forward, and if your future plans even include another horse.

Sometimes the path to your next horse is less direct and does not come through your own initiative. Having a new horse find you or having a horse brought to your attention when you don't undertake a search, may, for the lucky person, make the entire process of moving on much sooner than planned.

Robin Urciuoli was not looking for another horse when Bhenn entered her life:

> *A few weeks and countless tears after Alice died, I received a call from Kathy, my longtime friend and trainer. She had found a cute but very thin young Thoroughbred that she thought I might want to see. She couldn't explain why she told the dealer that he could leave the horse with her for a trial period—she really didn't have the room, and none of her students were looking for a green horse. Then she thought of me.*

> *I cried more tears than I thought I could possibly have left the night before I was supposed to go see this horse. How would I know if I should get him? Would Alice find a way to let me know her opinion? Would I be able to care for any other horse the way I had cared for Alice? Could I possibly get lucky enough to have something that would be as steady as Alice, or would I be tempting fate? I decided to at least go and try him so Kathy wouldn't have totally wasted her time.*

Later, when I got the news that this needy horse was mine, I started shaking, then made a list of things that would have to be done. I didn't feel right to be excited and it was too much to think of all the things I should fear, so I was stuck somewhere in the middle. No matter how corny it sounds, I felt Alice must have chosen this new horse, Bhenn, for me, but still wondered if he would ever recover from such severe neglect. Rehabbing Bhenn left little time for grief and watching him develop physically and mentally gave me something to enjoy.

It is important to realize that it is perfectly normal to have these feelings. It is also natural to bond with another animal and to want to move on to a new relationship. It does not mean that you love your deceased horse any less or that you are trying to move his or her memory out of your life. It is simply time for you to share your life with another animal.

Looking for a "Replacement"

Some people may have loved their horse so much that they try to find another "just like him or her." They may specifically look for an animal that physically resembles the lost horse in color, breed or markings. This can be a mistake as no two animals will be completely the same and, as such, the bond you share with each will be different. To place the burden of "measuring up" or "filling the shoes" of a former horse is unfair to a new mount and may cause you future disappointment, especially if the new mount does not measure up to your golden memories of your old horse. Your lost horse will always live on in your heart, so give this new horse a chance to earn your love in his or her own way.

Timing

Where the loss was a difficult one, it may take more than time to heal before you are ready to move on to your next horse. The process of finding your next animal may become a search for the "perfect" horse. Chasing perfection, yet never finding it, is another way of preserving the memory of your horse that is gone. Ruling out horses that do not meet your exhaustive list of selection criteria can, in some way, keep you from having to feel that you are doing something wrong in moving on to another horse, or that you are moving on to another horse too soon.

Some, as they search for their new horse, may look for some kind of guarantee or assurance that what happened to the last horse will not happen to the next horse. They may rule out good horses based on tiny flaws in a pre-purchase exam, for example, believing that it could spell disaster later on. And that may be entirely correct. There is nothing wrong with making a careful choice and basing your decision on concrete evidence. But when the process of making a choice becomes exceptionally difficult, it may be time to step back and consider whether you are ready for a new horse at this time in your life.

The old expression "timing is everything" applies in this situation. The time it takes to feel "ready" to love a new horse varies by individual. There is no right or wrong answer and if searching for—and not finding—the "perfect" horse brings the owner to her next horse in a roundabout way, so be it.

Renewing a Bond

If you already own another horse, you may choose this time to strengthen or renew that bond. For Kat Hampton, the death of her horse, Val, led to a renewed relationship with her second horse—one that was more difficult and challenging than the horse she lost:

> Lexie came into my life more than a year before Val died. Her owner and breeder had too many pony youngsters and too little time, and I agreed to take her on as a training project. While I had put a lot of time into the scraggly 3 year-old over the past several months, we had not made much headway. Lexie was as spooky, flighty, herd bound and stubborn as they come. Even my husband didn't care much for her.

Normally, working with Lexie meant a long and frustrating training lesson that left both of us tired and frustrated. Afterwards, I would turn her back out and she would tear off across the pasture, screaming and bucking. I still cannot understand why I suddenly felt the urge to work with her on the day after Val died.

I chased Lexie halfway around the pasture in an effort to catch her, and led her into the paddock. I had already discovered that Lexie hated to be lunged on a line, and free lunging wasn't much better, but maybe — just maybe — today would be different. And it was.

As my husband watched Lexie following me around the paddock, matching my every move, he said, "Hon, somehow, I'm going to find the money to get that horse for you." All of the sudden I realized that I was falling in love with the mare. There would never be another Val, but on that day, Lexie had managed to help fill in the huge, empty hole in my heart. I realized that in a way, it was as if Lexie was Val's final gift to me.

Conclusion

Moving on to that next horse is a milestone for many people. It lets them chart a new course in their lives. It brings them joy and happiness and lets them return to places that used to be familiar to them, such as barns, horse shows and tack shops. Having a horse takes time and commitment, and many horse owners find themselves centering their lives around their horses. A new horse restores to them a part of their routine that they had lost. The next horse may help to return its owner to that feeling of being centered and part of a bigger world. How quickly that happens is up to each individual.

Beyond the Rainbow Bridge

As much as I loved the life we had, of happiness and fun,
I reached the end of my life and knew my time on earth was done.
I saw a wondrous image then of a place that's trouble-free
Where all of us can meet again to spend eternity.

I saw the most beautiful rainbow, and on the other side
Were pastures rich and beautiful — lush and green and wide.
And running through these fields as far as the eye could see
Were horses and ponies of every sort as healthy as could be.
My own exhausted body was fresh and healed and new
And I wanted to gallop off with them, but had something left to do.

I needed to reach out to you, to tell you I'm alright
That this place is truly wonderful, then a bright glow pierced the night.
'Twas the glow of many candles shining bright and strong and bold
And I knew it held your love in all its brilliant shades of gold.

For although we're not together in the way we used to be,
We are still connected by something no eye can ever see.
So whenever you need to find me, we're never far apart
If you look beyond the Rainbow Bridge and listen with your heart.

— Author Unknown

RESOURCES

There are numerous books, pet loss support hotlines, groups and Web sites available to comfort individuals who have lost a horse. Below are just a few such options. Many others are available by searching the Internet or by contacting your veterinarian.

Books

Pet Loss: A Thoughtful Guide for Adults and Children by Herbert A. Nieburg and Arlene Fisher. Harper and Row, 1982.

Coping With Sorrow on the Loss of Your Pet by Moira K. Anderson. Peregrine Press, 1987.

When Only the Love Remains: The Pain of Pet Loss by Emily Margaret Stuparyk. Hushion House Publishing Ltd., 2000.

Goodbye, Friend: Healing Wisdom for Anyone Who Has Ever Lost a Pet by Gary Kowalski. Stillpoint Publishing, 1997.

Saying Good-Bye to the Pet You Love: A Complete Resource to Help You Heal by Lorri A. Greene and Jacquelyn Landis. New Harbinger Publications, 2002.

Pet Loss Support Hotlines

The following is a small sampling of pet loss hotlines. Information on many other hotlines is available by searching online.

Cornell Pet Loss Support Hotline: (607)253-3932
Web site: web.vet.cornell.edu/public/petloss/

Iowa State University Pet Loss Support Hotline: (888) 478-7574
Web site: www.vetmed.iastate.edu/animals/petloss

Tufts University Pet Loss Support: 508-839-7966
Web site: www.tufts.edu/vet/petloss/

University of Illinois Pet Loss Support Hotline: (877) 394-CARE (2273)
Web site: http://www.ourpals.com/support/memorial.htm

General Pet Loss Support Web sites

The following Web sites offer forums and resources on coping with pet loss. Many others may also be viewed online.

www.petloss.com
www.rainbowsbridge.com
www.pet-loss.net

Memorials

The following Web sites offer various gravestones, benches, urns, and other types of pet memorials for sale. Many others may also be viewed online.

www.foreverpets.com
www.allaboutpeturns.com
www.rainbowbridgepetmemorials.com
www.ourpals.com/support/memorial.htm

NOTES

1. Acquired online via interview from Cindy Sydnor to Kimberly Gatto, 2004.

2. Excerpts from "Misty" by Kimberlee Quarles, reprinted with kind permission of the American Association of Equine Practitioners.

3. Interview between Lendon Gray and Lisa Carusone, January 2005.

4. Excerpts from "Molly" by Tannetta Dow, originally published in **An Apple a Day**, reprinted with permission of Half Halt Press.

5. Excerpts from "Irish" by DeeDee Hunter, originally published in **An Apple A Day**, reprinted with permission from Half Halt Press.

6. Interview between Debi Metcalfe and Lisa Carusone, January 2005.

7. Excerpts from "Remembering Calypso" by Nancy Jaffer, reprinted with permission of Nancy Jaffer and Equisearch.com.

ABOUT THE AUTHOR

Kimberly Gatto is professional writer and the author of several books, including *An Apple A Day: A Heartwarming Collection of True Horse Stories* as well as biographies of sports stars Michelle Kwan, Emmitt Smith and Tom Brady. She is an honors graduate of Wheaton College and Boston Latin School. Kim's additional writing credits include articles in *Chronicle of the Horse, Sidelines* and *Chicken Soup for the Horse Lover's Soul.* Kim also wrote the foreword to Mona Goldstein's *No Hurdle Too High: The Story of Showjumper Margie Goldstein Engle.*

Kim is a lifelong horse owner who enjoys spending time with her two Thoroughbreds, Chutney and Grace, and competing at local horse shows. She is also a 4-H youth horse club leader. &

CONTRIBUTING EDITOR

Lisa Keer Carusone is a certified equine massage therapist, trained by Mike Scott, a nationally known therapist, teacher, and author. Lisa's Weston Equine Massage serves the needs of hard-working (and not so hard-working) horses and the owners who love them in greater New England. When not seeing clients, Lisa writes for several equine publications and provides web content and writing services for the equine industry.

A dressage rider, Lisa owns Telaraña, a young Andalusian/Hanoverian mare bred and started by Paul Belasik. Lisa lives in Weston, Massachusetts with her husband John, dogs Solo and Chloe, and cat Anabel.

CONTRIBUTORS

Equine artist **John Bellucci** has been photographing, painting portraits and sculpting the horse since 1973. John writes, "Having been around some of the greatest horses in recent history has been my inspiration, and the reason I consider the Thoroughbred racehorse one of the greatest and most honest athletes in the world. I am honored to know them!"

Rachel Bigger has been riding since she was 6 years old and is the current owner of two horses: Flirt, a Thoroughbred, and Filly, a Paint cross. Rachel works as a Web designer and currently trains and rides dressage. She aspires to ride at the FEI level and to breed and train her own upper level horse.

Kaylie Chaffee is fourteen years old and has been riding since she was ten. Kaylie is currently helping a friend train her horse and is slowly getting back into riding on a regular basis. Kaylie is an active member of 4-H and was recently elected Vice President of her club.

Jody Davidson is a published and professionally produced playwright whose works include adaptations of *If You Give A Mouse A Cookie, Black Beauty: The Musical, Snow Child, and Bitty Bear's Family Tree,* which is currently running at the American Girl Theatres in New York and Chicago. Jody has had a life-long love of all things equine and has recently returned to riding after a six year lay-off (while she supported her daughter's junior career!). Though she breeds several horse foals each year, Jody loves ponies and always has several new homebred or discovered prospects coming up through the show ranks. Her Web site is appropriately named www.perfectponies.com.   ◅

LR Davidson is now a college student studying opera at a noted conservatory in New York. She continues to ride as her school schedule permits and avidly shows, primarily in the High and Low Amateur-Owner Jumper divisions. LR and her mother Jody continue to breed, train and show ponies together.   ◅

Lendon Gray is the winner of more national dressage championships than any other rider in the U.S. She represented the U.S. at the 1978 World Championships and the 1991 World Cup as well as the 1980 and 1988 Olympics. Lendon also wrote a monthly series of training articles in *Practical Horseman* and is the author of the book **Lessons with Lendon**. She is the founder of Dressge4Kids, Inc. a non-profit organization whose mission is to provide quality educational and competitive events for America's young riders.   ◅

Kat Hampton lives in Georgia with her husband Tommy and their young son, Tyler, along with several horses, dogs, cats, and other animals. Kat has been riding for over 20 years. She has shown hunters, jumpers and dressage, and has galloped horses at the racetrack. Kat hopes to one day breed sport ponies.   ◅

Amanda Hogan is the executive director of Windrush Farm Therapeutic Equitation, Inc. in Boxford and North Andover Massachusetts. WFTE, Inc. is a NARHA Premiere Accredited non-profit therapeutic riding program that specializes in working with emotionally, mentally and physically challenged individuals of all ages. Mandy has been involved in the program for over 30 years. She is a licensed riding instructor, a NARHA master instructor and is involved in developing curriculum for Equine Facilitated Mental Health Association. Mandy is involved in the equine industry and is an active competitor in dressage and eventing with her daughter, Brie.   ◅

Jennifer E. King, DVM is a veterinarian with New England Horse Care Center in North Smithfield, Rhode Island. Dr. King is a graduate of Iowa State University College of Veterinary Medicine, and completed an internship at the Mid-Atlantic Equine Medical Center in New Jersey in 2002.She is a member of the AAEP, the Rhode Island Veterinary Medical Association, and the American Veterinary Medical Association. Dr. King is licensed to practice in Rhode Island, Massachusetts and Connecticut.   ᖍ

John Lyons has been recognized as "The Most Trusted Horseman in America" as a major clinician and speaker at the major horse expos and events across the country. Over the last 23 years John has traveled nationally and internationally, giving hands-on training clinics, demonstrations, symposiums, expos, seminars, lectures, etc. John has written 17 different books over a period of 10 years and has produced 27 videotapes on training, as well as 10 audiotapes.   ᖍ

Kimberly Maloomian started riding at the early age of 3 and began showing by the time she was 4. After showing Kim and Blue, she moved on to the junior hunter division aboard Greylock, whom she qualified for Devon, Harrisburg and Madison Square Garden in the large junior hunters, and Gypsy Gold, who earned her ribbons at Devon and Harrisburg in the small juniors. Presently, Kimberly trains with Mitch Steege of Red Acre Farm, competing in the adult hunter and equitation divisions. In May of 2005 she earned a degree in Information Design and Corporate Communication from Bentley College.   ᖍ

Ashlee Mansour is a single mother who attempts to balance work, family and horses. After riding horses as a child, Ashlee returned to the sport as an adult. Through her horse Parade, Ashlee was able to share her love of horses with her young son.   ᖍ

Amy Neal trains horses and riders at her Cornerstone Farm in Massachusetts. Amy has competed successfully in both the western pleasure and hunter divisions with her Arabian gelding, Silver Sent. Amy and her husband Mike are the proud parents of two young sons, Randy and Zachary.   ✑

One of the foremost and respected horsemen in the world, **Lynn Salvatori Palm** of Palm Partnership Training is a pioneer among women in the horse industry. For more than 30 years, Lynn has championed the partnership of horse and rider, bringing her unique perspective to hundreds of thousands of horse enthusiasts around the world. Lynn holds a record four American Quarter Horse Association Super Horse titles and 34 World and Reserve World championships.   ✑

Nancy Pemberton lives in Tryon, North Carolina, with her horses, border terriers, and pet conure (bird). She has recently begun a second career in real estate in order to support the general livestock population.   ✑

Jennifer Shirey is a software consultant for a health information systems company and has been riding for much of her life. Skippy was her first horse after a long "horse hiatus." Author's Note: Jenni has recently become the proud owner of Leo, a beautiful chestnut Thoroughbred gelding.   ✑

Jill Swift is an event rider and trainer with over 12 years of experience in the horse industry. She teaches children and adults at all levels in eastern Massachusetts. Jill holds a bachelor's degree in Psychology from Boston College, and lives in Leominster, Massachusetts with her husband, Dave, and their dog, Mabel.   ✑

Cindy Sydnor is an accomplished dressage rider and trainer. After seven years in Europe and Brazil, Cindy returned to the U.S. in 1972 and was long-listed for the 1976 U.S. Olympic Team and stayed on the USET "long list" for several years. She has competed nationally at all levels and continues to do so. She is an "R" dressage judge and an examiner for the USDF Instructor Certification Program. Cindy has trained eight horses from the start to Intermediaire and three to the Grand Prix. She currently trains horses and riders at all levels from her home in Snow Camp, North Carolina. Cindy and her husband Charles Sydnor have three children.   ∽

Robin Urciuoli is a licensed riding instructor and a certified public accountant. Robin lives in Massachusetts, where she enjoys competing in hunters and dressage with her horse, Meant To Be (a.k.a. "Bhenn").   ∽

Doris J. Worcester, is a Licensed Independent Clinical Social Worker and Certified Cognitive Behavioral Therapist who specializes in performance coaching for equestrian clients. Through her practice, The Performance Edge, Doris helps riders of all disciplines and skill levels to create deeper partnerships with their horses and to successfully achieve their equestrian dreams. As a result, Doris is very familiar with the bond between horse and rider and the psychological and emotional impact of this relationship loss. A rider herself, Doris competes in the Hunter/Jumper division in New England on her Irish Sport Horse, Quarter Time.

Maureen van der Stad is Doris' friend and was kind enough to share SoBo's story with us.   ∽